Boxing Day

Raymond Fraser Buchanan

Grosvenor House
Publishing Limited

The right of Raymond Fraser Buchanan to be identified as the author of this
work has been asserted in accordance with Section 78
of the Copyright, Designs and Patents Act 1988

This book is published by
Grosvenor House Publishing Ltd
Link House
140 The Broadway, Tolworth, Surrey, KT6 7HT.
www.grosvenorhousepublishing.co.uk

A CIP record for this book
is available from the British Library

ISBN 978-1-80381-263-2
eBook ISBN 978-1-80381-264-9

PROLOGUE

A remarkable true story of courage in the face of adversity where dreams come true.

The bones of this story will resonate with millions of people all over the world.

ACKNOWLEDGEMENTS

THIS BOOK IS DEDICATED TO

Allana, Charli and Skyla

With special thanks

Anne Grzybowski, Sonia Lynn, Ian Stewart, Jimmy Pace, Jane Cormack and everyone who believed in me.

Also with thanks to Julie Scott of Grosvenor House Publishing

IN LOVING MEMORY OF ROSE AND ED

Chapter 1

We were just two kids in the back garden wearing boxing gloves.

"I'm Ken Buchanan, you're Muhammad Ali."

"Fuck off! I'm Ken Buchanan, you're Muhammad Ali."

"You fuck off."

There's been a miraculous amount of ifs and buts gone through my head from beginning to present day that warps my head in an ongoing spiral of constant confusion. What lay ahead for me was a manifestation of a wild dream that turned out to be real.

1970, Prestonpans, near Edinburgh, Scotland. I was being violently abused, both physically and mentally. Dragged by the hair behind the door – I could feel my hair being dragged out by the roots – kicked, punched, beaten up. The bar of soap rammed down my throat almost killed me. I was within an inch of my life, gagging that hard I felt sick from the effort I summoned to keep me alive. The soap residue was dripping inside my air passage that kept me breathing. My life flashed before my eyes, just for that second, I thought I was dead. While behind the door, these words would resonate through my mind like it was yesterday.

"I'll be a good boy, please let me out."

I still get nightmares to this day.

After the initial beatings, I was on the receiving end of one last frenzied attack that essentially put me in hospital. I knew this final onslaught happened on Boxing Day. The person who did this was someone who hated my real father.

Before these incomprehensible acts of ludicrous nonsense happened to a child who knew very little about the substance of life, I fell in love with boxing. My hero was Ken Buchanan.

These words kept resounding in my ear.

"I'll be a good boy, please let me out. I'll be a good boy, please let me out."

Chapter 2

On the way home, I let out a silent cry. On arrival, I sat on the floor, writhing in pain. It felt like a lifetime. Then I was in a hospital bed. The ward was long and spacious. It was almost empty, apart from someone far down the other side. A lady asked how I got there; she was really friendly. I started to tell her, then Roseanne entered the room.

"Don't listen to him."

The lady went away. All I could think about was how I got there. My leg was black and blue, I could feel lumps on my head. Roseanne wanted me to commit to a contract, hypothetically written in blood and hatred.

"If you don't tell anyone, we'll bring you up."

"So, I'll not go to the orphanage?"

"No, you'll be our son."

There was no room for negotiation. Roseanne and Eddie were nice people, they wouldn't hurt a fly. They could argue, even a wee kid like me could just about manage to referee their private altercations. I'd rather take my chances with them. I was just a young kid, what else could I do.

"Okay, I promise."

"You'll get John's bed, son."

"Okay."

I'd slept in a cot for almost five years. It had bars to keep you in, I felt like a caged animal. This would be a massive step in the right direction, it was luxury. It's unreal to think the first time I slept in a proper bed was in hospital, right there, right then.

They swiftly took me to another hospital in Edinburgh called Douglas House, where my leg was put in plaster. One minute I was lying in a hospital bed, next thing my plastered leg was hanging suspended in the air for months. I found a way to lower the cast, I got one of the boys to loosen the traction, it was a proper laugh. The nurses were mystified. This smartly dressed man came in, gave me jumping beans from America, the beans never jumped. I was more interested in watching *Scooby Doo* on the telly. The doctors said I may never walk properly again; I may never kick a ball or even enter a boxing ring. That was as good as it got. I was the only one in the ward with my leg in the air wearing a full cast. I never thought too much about it at the time, I was more interested in *Scooby Doo*, and shouting at the boys sitting in front of the telly.

"Fuck off! Get out the way."

The cast was on so long, it was brutal. My leg got so itchy, only God knows how much time went by. It was like being trapped, it was a nightmare, it was hell. I've no idea how long I'd been lying there, it had to be months. I lost track of time, days became weeks, weeks became months. They eventually took the cast off, although I had to stay in bed. One night I was constantly swearing, the nurses lifted me upstairs and put me in a room full of babies, it was murder. All I could hear was babies screaming, it was driving me nuts. Eventually I was taken back downstairs to my own bed, that was a weird night. I'd spent so long in a cast; it was nobody's business. I started to walk again using a caliper, parallel bars to assist me. Then I progressed to walking in a straight line. I was only allowed to get out of bed for two hours a day. I spent a few days scribbling on a jotter before they realised I hadn't started school. Roseanne visited me when she could, it was a long way from Prestonpans. On the day they let me go home, Roseanne told me one of my legs was slightly shorter than the other. I'd rather be alive than dead at the hands of that monster.

John had an immaculate bed; it was really comfy. It was comforting to know I was safe; it was great to be back in Prestonpans. I still loved watching boxing; my hero was the champion of the world. I couldn't dance around, punching Eddie's hands anymore. John couldn't slap me on the legs for taking more than my fair share of the couch. He would visit twice a year. Maria went on holiday as much as she could. You never saw much of Maria, she always made me smile.

My vocabulary was rapidly expanding on account of the lessons I was receiving next door in Auntie Anna's kitchen. When it came to cooking chips, Anna's were the best in the world. Her son, Kevin, and I would stand there in appreciation while Anna served us chips.

"You think this is a bed and breakfast, ya little cunt, you'll eat the fucking lot. Does that cunt through there no' feed ye, fucking terrible!"

Anna was describing how hungry I was. I would stand there with Kevin, half a chip hanging out my mouth nodding my head.

"The bairn's fucking starving. Look at him, Kevin, it's a fucking scandal. I've never heard the likes, give him more chips."

Anna had a way with words, she could tell I loved her cooking. Kevin and I would divide the remaining chips, and we'd race to see who could eat them first.

"Away to buck, the little cunt's ate the fucking lot."

Anna appreciated my love of her cooking.

"Thanks, Anna."

Eyes staring at the chip basket.

"Want more! Al fucking give ye more. Would you look at it, you'd think it hadn'y fucking seen a bite to eat, look at the een on it."

Anna was referring to my eyeballs staring out my head. Anna was an angel without wings, the aura that surrounded her was bursting with love. She had four kids of her own but treated every kid like one of her own, and she always gave you a kiss on the lips.

The street we lived in was called Gardiner Road, it was known locally as Finian Alley. We'd watch the bands marching from the bottom of the street, the bands were great fun. Some of the boys had proper sticks fitted with a mace, using red, white and blue sellotape. You'd be lying if you didn't envy them. Roseanne was very fierce about not giving me a lend of her brush. Sometimes I'd get a loan of a brush, it was magic trying to copy the guy in front of the band. There was a real sense of euphoria when the brush got thrown in the air, it was harder to judge than a proper stick, sometimes it whacked you on the head. It didn't matter what religion you were; everyone was at it. Everyone wanted a proper stick; everyone wanted a mace.

I still played football wearing my caliper, but it wasn't the same. I liked to race with my pals, they would give me a start. I was going to win this race when my caliper springs broke, the springs were crucial. They stopped me from putting weight on my left leg, the whole contraption lay at the mercy of the springs. I crawled a few yards on my hands and knees and slapped the finish line in first place. Roseanne would carry me home. There was only one shop in Edinburgh that sold caliper springs. Roseanne had to get a few buses there and back, sometimes I'd be sitting on the couch for days.

Brian Cochrane was thirteen, he had an adult's bike, he gave me a shot of it one day. I pedaled around the block using my right foot, I could hardly touch the pedal, half the journey was along a main road with cars and buses. It was dangerous, I liked dangerous, I was a daredevil, it was great, I felt alive. Brian had faith in me, he trusted me with his bike, I trusted him, we pulled off a minor miracle.

Roseanne would lift me into a pushchair and put my caliper on at the school gates. Half the street walked along with us, it was comforting in many ways. Entering the school was another matter. I could feel people staring at me, whispering, and pointing. I took a seat near the front of the class. All the boys had gathered at the back, discussing who was the bully. I hastily rushed to the back of the class, knocking into chairs and tables.

"What does bully mean?"

"The hardest."

"That's me! I'm the hardest!"

"You cannae be the hardest, you're a cripple.'

"I'll cripple you, ya cunt."

The first three years shared a playground, Paul Smith was being lauded as the hardest. Before hospital, I'd play kicking games in Finian Alley, Paul always ran away from me.

I sat in the nearest seat for registration.

"Raymond Fraser!"

"Fuck off!"

It was a strict Roman Catholic school; I was getting the belt on a daily basis. There was a dyke at the back of the playground, not many people could climb it, I managed it with a caliper. Walking along was extremely dangerous. It led onto an even bigger wall that separated the playground from a building site. I climbed that wall also. The top of the wall was much narrower than the last. I walked halfway along, then wouldn't come down. All the teachers were out, it was dangerous, the headmaster was offering me sweeties, the police turned up, even Roseanne. I stood on that wall for a long time. When I decided to come down, it was straight to the headmaster's office. Jocky Reynolds was a stocky, built man who could lay the belt, he asked me to choose between three of them. I kept pulling my hands away before the belt would make contact. He straddled himself across me, forced out my arms, then started lashing away, hitting hands, arms, and legs.

I felt ostracized from my class, I was the odd one out in many ways. All I done was fight and get the belt every day. The teacher made me sit at the front of the class. It had its benefits; I could trip people up with my caliper. Winter was hard, wearing a caliper in the snow. Roseanne was no longer using the pushchair, she was no longer dropping me off, I made the journey on my own. When a spring broke on my caliper, I'd sit down 'til Roseanne rescued me.

I missed lots of days at school due to the caliper, I fell behind reading *Janet and John* books, my writing was abysmal. Nobody in the house helped me with my reading and writing, nobody helped me with homework full stop. I hated school, hated being tormented by kids who never knew any better. Most of all, I hated the teachers for scolding me with a leather strap, it was embarrassing, mental torture. The only thing I had to look forward to was watching boxing on the telly. I was a fighter, I wanted to be a boxer just like my hero, for the time being, I was Hop-along the Cripple. Kids can be so cruel.

Chapter 3

We moved to a house in Polwarth Terrace, it was closer to the school, it was on the one level, it was more convenient for Roseanne, especially with me having a caliper. The street was quiet compared to Gardiner Road. Roseanne, Eddie and I stayed in there at first, I got a room to myself. John was still in Cyprus; Maria had got her own house. It was great while it lasted; for a brief period of time I had my own room, and for that moment in time I had a room that was free of smoke, I enjoyed the moment, it gave my young, developing lungs a break, it was a blessing.

After a year wearing a caliper, I was free from the shackles that held me back. I'd gradually went from two hours of walking, to complete freedom, it was a miracle, I was so happy, I was told to take it easy, on doctor's orders. The day I was free to roam the playground, 1 got my revenge on the name-callers, lots of people were amazed I wasn't a cripple anymore, I'd stuck to the rules, I had my legs back. There was an older guy who lived at the top of Polwarth Terrace who would call me vile names every day, I caught up with him that day, punched him through a hedge, he never said a bad word to me again.

The wanderer returned; John came back from Cyprus, he'd been intercepting Morse code for the Royal Signals. He took up 99%of the front room we shared, he had a wardrobe, set of drawers, he sat at a big desk sending Morse code signals all over the world, his posters adorned every wall. I had a single bed that the Harkness family were throwing out, right behind the door, right in the corner. The smell of smoke in my bedroom was disgusting, he wouldn't open a window, not even a crack, all I could breathe was this thick, heavy, dirty, smoke. Living in that house was like an endurance test, it should have come with a health warning. I was too young to notice before, now I could feel it breaking me down. In the evening, I took my chances in the living room with Roseanne puffing away, telling stories about the war, about the blackouts, when aircraft bombers were hovering above, trying to eliminate the nearby power station, covering the windows with dark sheets, candlelit rooms. She could talk for hours about the war, I listened carefully. Eddie was quiet, he just sat there smoking his pipe.

On the run up to school sports day, some of the boys in my class had joined running clubs, they all wanted to win the sprint, they wanted to win everything, it became very competitive. I'd been told to take it easy, I wasn't exerting myself, I wasn't competing in practice runs. The teachers told me I couldn't take part in sports day, I was gutted, I wanted to race, I wanted to compete, I felt really sad. At home, I expressed my feelings to Roseanne. She understood my frustration, she was well aware of what the doctors said, I wanted to take part, I wanted to compete, all I asked for was a chance, she told me she'd do her best. Roseanne confronted the teachers, put them in their place, I could swear the building started to shake, she was a force to be reckoned with, she wouldn't take no for an answer. I took a pair of training shoes with me to school on sports day, Roseanne was there to lay down the law, she was an immaculate force of nature, I was allowed to compete, nobody was going to argue with Roseanne. I lined up for the sprint, took off like a shot being fired from a gun, never stopped running at the finish line, never stopped 'til I reached the janitor's house. I'd won the race, I won every race, I proved the teachers wrong, I was a competitor, I was a winner.

As a child, I mostly hung around with Kevin Clelland, Jamie Adams and Ricky Adams. Jamie and Kevin were two years older than Ricky and me, Ricky and Jamie were brothers, Kevin had been my next-door neighbour in Gardiner Road. We played lots of football, we always played against older boys, it was great fun, it was tough, I loved every minute. Big Kenny Stevenson could half you in two with a tackle. We played toy fighting, I'd easily get Ricky to the ground, I'd easily drag Jamie off Kevin. I seemed to like fighting, it was evident that fighting was my forte, none of them would put the boxing gloves on, none of them could handle me. They wanted to be footballers, I wanted to fight my hero, Ken Buchanan. We'd run a lot, we'd run from orchards, we'd run from people who owned orchards, all we wanted was apples, something to eat, something to fill our bellies, something to fuel us up, just a piece of nature's gift.

All the boys were calling each other cousin. It was the first time I'd heard anyone use that word, it had played on my mind, I asked Roseanne if I had any cousins.

"Everyone's your cousin."

It was comforting to hear that, it was a relief, a strong sense of belonging. That was the first time I felt safe in the knowledge I wasn't alone; we were all part of something much bigger. It triggered brain cells in my head that I'd continually carry, it triggered hope, I was doped up with feelings of excitement, the winds of belonging carried me a long way. I had grown in confidence since getting the caliper off, nothing could stop me.

At school, Victor introduced me to the Pope. He wasn't ordained, he didn't have a pointy hat, he didn't wear fine silks, he was in the year above me, his real name was Paul Garrity, and everyone called him Pope. He always told the truth, there was nothing up his sleeve, what you saw is what you got. He was a real pal, I'm glad I met the Pope, he played a significant part in shaping my future, he came through for me at a time when nobody else cared.

Kevin, Jamie, Ricky and I walked to Port Seton open-air swimming pool. It was a hot day, by the time we got to Cockenzie High Street we were parched, desperate for a drink, almost delirious. The old lady in Cockenzie High Street seemed like a mirage, she was handing out precious glasses of water, satisfying our thirst. It was an act of kindness, she could see we were in distress, she had a fountain of cold water, she was our saviour. On entrance to the pool, you got a band and a metal basket. We sang on our way to the changing rooms, we sang it in the changing rooms, shouting at the top of our voice.

"Cody! Cody! Come or die young, hello! Hello!"

It was Brian Cochrane's gang, he was the leader, he made the whole thing up, we were believers, Cody was Prestonpans, Prestonpans was Cody. It was intimidating going into the changing rooms, we had a chant to protect us from all evil, we were armed to the teeth in vocal spirit, we had something to protect us, we had Cody. We saved our bus fares by walking, and we went to the Italian cafe on the corner, it was a lovely little place that sold beautiful ice cream, the cream was so tasty, it was worth walking for, it was the best treat in the world, apart from Anna's chips.

All my class moved to the next, they tried to hold me back, my reading and writing was well below standard. Nobody in the house helped with homework, nobody cared if I did it, so I never did it. I could hardly write; I could hardly read. I got held back for two weeks, then Roseanne threatened to pull the building down. They quickly moved me to the next class. All the boys fancied Pamela Dixon, I fancied the teacher, she was young, slim, long brown hair, you could say I liked Miss Souter. She was different, she could never belt me, I don't know why. Every other teacher had two chances each, I hated them, I hated getting the belt. I swore too much, it was the way I got brought up, I could swear before I spoke a broad, Scottish east coast slang. Every word that came out my mouth was, "Fuck off!"

A boy in my class had leukemia, his name was Brian Hogg, we sometimes walked home together, he was a lovely guy, intelligent, well mannered. He wore a wig to school after the treatment kicked in, some kids made fun of him, he got a lot of abuse in the playground, Gerry took care of him for the most part, on occasion I had to step in to render someone horizontal. Brian went to a place in France called Lourdes, it was a holy place where miracles had happened, he went there in hope of a miracle, we sent him a tape of our best wishes, his chances were low. He was a devout catholic, his family were deeply religious, truly a miracle did happen, he's still alive and well to this day.

I heard my hero had lost his world title, it was hard to believe, it was a low blow, the fight wasn't televised, it affected a nation, it affected me and all the other kids who idolized him. I was so sad Rosanne said my Uncle James wanted to give me a puppy. I went down to Aberlady to see the litter, I got first pick. Every pup my Uncle James said was a wee beauty I rejected, my eyes were drawn to this wee fella, he was so cute, just stared at me while the others jumped around, no matter what my uncle said, I had made my mind up – it was the wee fella. I was so happy with my puppy, I really thought I had a bit of company, he died after two days, it turned out he was the runt of the litter. So Roseanne bought me my favorite song on vinyl, 'Puppy Love' by Donny Osmond, I played it over and over, that many times I scratched the vinyl, it became unplayable, these lyrics kept resounding in my ear.

Someone, help me, help me, help me please...
Is the answer up above...
How can I, oh, how can I tell them...?
This is not a puppy love, not a puppy love...

Chapter 4

A couple of classmates, Matty Bowes and Sandy Costello, lived in Port Seton. They had to walk past the Protestant school on the way home. They had been getting bullied by the Protestants, kicked, punched and verbally abused and spat on. I volunteered to help them; I was always fighting everyone else battles so didn't seem like a big deal. On the way to the bus stop, we were getting abuse hurled from the Protestants.

"Fenian bastards."

They charged at us. I was incited with rage, so I charged back, decking the first boy I came into contact with. I was punching my way through them, the rest of them backed away.

"No' fucking big men now, eh?"

I was going off my head. This boy got up. I leathered him again, chased him halfway up the road. Matty and Sandy told me I'd got the ringleader. After some time walking them down the road, the Protagonists got the message and my mates never got bothered again.

At weekends I'd walk down to Matty's, just past Cockenzie power station. We'd play in the small harbor, observe the small fishing boats that were getting mended or just ashore, and play in the park across from his house on the corner next to Port Seton British Legion. It was there I met one of Matty's friends named Colin. He was older than us and supposedly the hardest in his class. He was acting like a ticket, shouting about how he done karate. I had to say something. "Fuck off!"

Colin kept backing off, then jumped the wall to get away.

Matty kept ferrets for pets, or that's was what I thought – his dad used them for catching rabbits. Matty had his hand in the cage, petting Whitey. He told me they were really soft, friendly creatures, Whitey was pure white, white as the driven snow. Whitey was being so loving and affectionate to him, they looked friendly enough creatures to me. His dad shouted, "Stay away from the cages, son."

This didn't deter Matty. He was now asking me just to poke my finger threw the cage. The beast had looked friendly enough with him, I thought it would be harmless just to stroke the wee fella's head, so I poked my finger threw the cage and started to stroke Whitey's head. I was petting the ferret for a while until I touched his nose. "Ya fucking bastard!" The ferret sunk its teeth into my index finger, it had a strong grip, I couldn't pull my finger out the cage. "Let go, ya fuckin' cunt!"

Matty's dad rushed out the back door, opened the cage and somehow managed to release its jaws, the blood was dripping everywhere. I was in panic mode; this was a shock to the system. "Fuck you, Matty!"

His dad told me to stay where I was, I just wanted to get home, so I started walking away, then running. His dad was running after me with bandages, but I was stopping for no one. "Fuck off!"

I ran like the wind, I ran like Usain Bolt, my heart was beating out my chest,

It was cold in the winter wearing shorts, some of the boys even had gloves. Gordon Purves had a pair, he left one behind when the bell to signal the end of playtime went off. Sparky thought it would be funny if we shoved a bit of dog shit into his glove using sticks. Gordon got a nasty surprise, Sparky blamed it on me, and I got the belt again from the headmaster.

We went to Tranent indoor swimming pool. We'd walk across the bing and up the Shough to Tranent. The Shough was like a valley with trees on either side, you were taking a chance going that way, it was where the Belters would play. 'Belters' was what the Tranent people were called, we were called Panners and Prestonpans was called the Pans. We lived less than a mile apart but fought like cats and dogs. It was all new to me but I'd do anything to save money on bus fares so I could get a bag of strawberry bonbons after the swimming. I learnt to swim that day, someone pushed me on the back while I was sizing up the deep end, kicking my feet and doing the doggy paddle with my hands kept me afloat. Within no time I was lashing away with my arms and paddling with my feet, I'd watched Tarzan doing the same on telly. Six years old and I was swimming like a fish in no time.

At Port Seton open air swimming pool, the high dive was the highest in Scotland 'til they built a bigger one at Portobello. We would all bounce off the springboard no bother, but none of my mates would go near it. I was a real daredevil, practically do anything within reason. I climbed the stairs to the sound of the boys shouting, "You'll never do it!"

That's when I realized I was scared of heights, but fuck it! I just took a run and jumped off. You were not supposed to jump, the lifeguard never saw me, so I got away with it.

When I was seven, I'd go to watch Kevin play for Tranent Legion Club under 10s. I began to take my football boots with me in case they were a player short, Kevin told me to do it. I was a striker but came on against Whitecraig as a substitute playing left back, although I was right-footed. I wanted to score goals, this guy from the opposing team called Paddy Neilson kept slipping the ball past me and ran right by. Paddy was fast, he also had the momentum to run straight past me. I was having to turn around and chase him, I knew right there and then I was definitely not a defender. I went with the team to a safari park where we saw lots of wild animals.

And we took a boat ride down a narrow river, then had lunch.

The best part was Tranent Gala. The Legion had a float in the parade. People were throwing money onto the float; it was a lorry decorated in the British Legion colours. My bucket was starting to fill up when this guy called Darren Fynan informed me, "Put half in your bucket and half in your pocket, everyone's doing it, pal."

It didn't feel right putting money in my pocket but everyone else was doing it, so I started to fill the linings of my trousers with money that people were throwing onto the float. In the end, I had a bucket full of money and two bulging pockets. It was a great day; my face was like a laughing tomato handing over the bucket. There was no way I could hide the money I'd stuffed in my pockets. Nobody paid attention, they just took the buckets at the end of the day. Kevin and I walked down to the Pans loaded. I'll never forget that day. Darren and I had spent a lot of time that season talking on the sideline as substitutes, but we had reaped the benefits at the gala day parade. Kev and I felt like kings. It had got to the stage at one point we were putting copper coins in the buckets and silver ones in our pockets.

I never got pocket money. It was good to go into Tommy Morgan's sports shop and buy new studs for playing on soft ground, shorter ones for hard ground. I had money to go swimming and the cinema in Musselburgh. Just for a wee while I felt rich. All I would get for a snack in the house was rich tea biscuits and digestives Monday to Saturday and Bourbon creams on a Sunday, that was the nearest the I got to chocolate, but not now – I could buy a toffee cup, but when the money ran out it was back to rich tea and digestives. Roseanne always made stew every day for tea and the same for Sunday dinner, it was constant. We never got a dessert – the Bourbon creams came out. I loved ice cream, never really saw much. Lots of my mates got a pudding, some of them got ice cream, my pudding was as close to chocolate as you could get, but not quite the real deal – a Bourbon cream.

Roseann loved pan drops; they were cheap, round, white mints, shaped like a kind of flying saucer, I often had one or two. They brought out new ones that were not regular size, these were giant pan drops that were sold in singles. One day John gave Eddie and I one each while they were watching the telly. They were that big it consumed your mouth, you just had to persevere until it got smaller. I got it trapped in my throat, I couldn't breathe or speak, all I could do was make hand gestures to John and Eddie. John quickly lifted me by the ankles, Eddie continuously slapped my back. Eventually the giant pan drop fell on the floor. There was someone up there looking out for me. I never touched a giant pan drop again, I stuck to regular ones.

I got held back in primary two for the same reasons as primary one, reading and writing. Roseanne charged around to the school and I was moved up again. This time we were being taught by nuns. They asked us lots of general knowledge questions, Gerry O'Brian would answer them all. He was the brainiest in the class, he could read newspapers – I thought newspapers were for putting your dinner plate on. Gerrard would answer 99% of all questions, there wasn't much point in most of us being there. He was like a machine, like a modern-day computer, he had an answer for everything.

The nuns would have a go at belting me but most of the time they just brought in other teachers to do it for them. I couldn't walk away from fights, I was always fighting everyone else's battles, so it was business as usual, getting the belt every day.

Some boys in the class and would go down to Northfield Gardens to play with Pamela Dixon after school. Pamela was a great laugh, fun to be around. On the way down, the boys would practice kissing by touching their thumb and their first finger together, you always got a game of kiss catch. I had never kissed anyone in my life, not to my knowledge, my family were old-fashioned and set in their ways. At the end of the night, all the boys would stand in line for a goodnight kiss from Pamela. I stood on the other side of the road; I wouldn't do line-ups for a kiss.

Wearing shorts to school was murder in winter, snowball fights were stinging on your bare hands and freezing cold if you got hit on the legs.

You were allowed to bring games into class on the run up to Christmas holidays, most of the boys brought in draughts. I couldn't read or write properly but I was the only one in my class who could play chess. John had been teaching me to play since he got out the British Army.

Christmas Day started to become too predictable. Roseanne and Eddie would get me a Thursday market job Celtic strip and Celtic football annual; Maria would give me a fiver and John would present me with another pair of moccasins – they were essentially house slippers.

Roseanne caught me saying the word bastard, I never swore in the house, not with the big cross and Jesus hanging from it. She told me that was a bad word, never to use it ever again. I asked Gerry O'Brian what that word meant, he told me to look it up in the dictionary, I'd never used a dictionary before, I could hardly speak English. I finally found it in the dictionary: A person born of unmarried parents; an illegitimate child. This didn't make much sense to me, but I hammered anyone who called me it. I began to ask Roseanne if I could call her 'mum' and Eddie 'dad', all my friends had mum and dads. She said I could call her nana because nana's look after people. I'd been told I had loads of cousins, aunties and uncles, the only thing missing was a mum and dad. I was still seven years old, almost eight, shared a room with John who smoked the pipe all night. All I had in that room was a single bed. Roseanne and Eddie would be puffing away in the living room, there was no place I could do my homework, so I just accepted the strap of leather instead. They belted me for anything.

When the better weather came in, the nuns left and we got a teacher called Mrs Thane. She took us out to play rounders, it was a bit like baseball, but you used a tennis racket and ball. I was the first person to launch it over the chapel wall. Everyone who threw the ball at me was shitting themselves in case I hit them.

My eighth birthday came, I usually just got cards, it was not a big deal. However, Roseanne told me I could go to boxing when I was eight. This meant Maria coming down from Bonnyrigg to take me to a sports centre across from Woodburn Miners Club in Dalkeith. The first night there I was sparring, I copied my hero, I fought like Ken Buchanan. I stayed in the boxing ring and took on every boy around my age one at a time. Eddie was over at the miner's club using John's pass to get in for most of the night, but the trainer did ask him where I had boxed before. I was just copying my hero. I loved going to boxing training. John and Eddie would take it in turns to go with me, they spent most of the night over at the club rather than watch me. Sometimes they were still in the club when I was finished. I'd go downstairs, hang about the entrance to the disco. The kids who went there were all a lot older than me, I often wondered if Ken Buchanan had to do this. Eventually John or Eddie would show up, then Maria would pull into the car park and give us a lift home to the Prestonpans.

There was a show coming up and I wanted to be on it. I weighed the same as this guy who I'd been easily beating in sparring. He was going to the club a lot longer than me, so on the night he got the nod. I was raging, swearing my head off. Eddie couldn't control me as we took our seats. When the boy came on, I constantly shouted, "It should have been me, ya cunt!" I exploded at the top of my voice over and over. Eddie had to take me out the hall, that's how bad I was.

Maria stopped coming down to take me to boxing, it's all I'd wanted to do since I was three years old. It's all I wanted to do; I never got a chance. I'd never asked for anything in my life. This was the only thing I felt passionate about, the only thing I watched on the telly. I was really disappointed, gutted. I was eight years old and watched my dream disappear rapidly. Maria said it was too much bother for her to take me. All I wanted to do was box. I didn't think I was too much to ask, I didn't see a problem. I remember telling Kevin's big brother, Tam, that I wanted to fight Ken Buchanan. I was angry, Tam arranged a slap boxing match against a guy who was four years older than me in his front garden. You had to be careful where you put your feet because there was a diamond shape cut out the middle of the grass where they had flowers. I just kept slapping Archie in the face and moving away, he couldn't get near me. I was luring Archie nearer the diamond then stepped to the side, Archie had committed with a shot, then landed in the flowers, all the boys were laughing.

Three years on the trot I'd won every race at school sports day and I had a good season playing football for Tranent Legion Under 10s, scoring lots of goals as center forward.

Chapter 5

Roseanne took me on my first holiday to Barlanark in Glasgow. It was more like a weekend, a couple of days. It was not a normal holiday destination by any stretch of the imagination. There was no fun fair, tourist shops or people handing out flyers. It was just a big hill to climb and a row of old tenement flats. Uncle Pat's was at the top of the hill, the very last one, you could see his house from the motorway on the way coming in. Roseanne was toiling walking up the hill having to stop for a few breathers on the way.

My Uncle Pat was hilarious, always joking, always had plenty of time for you. When you were around Uncle Pat, life was just one big party. He was always laughing. He made you feel at home, like one of his own. He made me laugh so much, he could talk for Scotland and always with a smile on his face. It was amazing the energy and laughter there was in the same room as him.

I got to play with my cousin Pat McGuire. We would play on the football fields across from his house, climb up the walls of the adjacent school, and sit on the window ledges. At the foot of the street there was a newsagent, bookies and a pub.

We'd roam the streets 'til it was dark. Auntie Betty would make us something to eat. She always fussed over you, such a lovely woman inside and out. She was such an affectionate woman, she wouldn't let you go anywhere without giving you a big smacker on the lips, she reminded me of Auntie Anna, but Auntie Betty never swore.

It was hard leaving Barlanark, I had such a great time, I would rather go there than Butlin's any day of the week. You just seemed to fit in, it was the first time in my life I never felt like the odd one out. I kept staring back at Uncle Pat's house from the motorway, I even turned around in my seat until it was out of sight.

Eddie and I were craving for another dog, so Roseanne finally caved in and got us one. I called it Rover, this one lasted more than two days. Rover looked too big to be a pup, I could roll about with him, cuddle him and clapped him all night. This was a great summer, I was out playing football all day with Kevin, Jamie and Ricky, at night I gave my undivided attention to Rover. When I moved into Primary 4, he was always waiting at the gate for me coming home from school. I had the best of both worlds.

I was trying harder to listen to the teacher. There were three groups in class that were in accordance to which level of study you were at, I had been moved up to the middle group. We'd get sheets of paper with sums on them, all you had to do was fill in the answers. Gerry O'Brian was always first out to the teacher with his finished paper, I kind of got in a race to the teacher with Gerry. A lot of the time I managed to beat him but always made a couple of mistakes during the frantic race. Miss Thane had told me to take my time so I could complete my sheet of work with every question correct but I got more elation racing Gerry. It had become an obsession, I only wanted to be moved into the top group, being finished with my work first gave me more satisfaction though, I hated losing at anything, especially when John always beat me at chess.

Pamela had a birthday party, the only way I found out was because everyone was talking about the fighting that went on during the party. Brian Hogg, God love him, he was infatuated with Pamela. Anytime Pamela had to kiss anyone while playing a game he would start a fight. According to what I heard, it was pandemonium, everyone in the class was there. Supposedly, the reason I never got invited was because they thought that I would start a fight.

I did get invited to Gerry O'Brian's birthday party; Brian was under strict instructions not to cause any trouble. Gerry didn't live far from me, I'd walk home with him and Brian a lot, from where I lived it was six of one, and half a dozen of the other as to whether I walked the top or bottom road. We played that kissing game at Gerry's party. I was so shy with girls, the only females I had kissed were Auntie Anna and Auntie Betty and

I never had a choice in the matter, they would just plant one on me. The moment I was dreading finally came, all the girls had picked me to go behind the living room door and into the hall, all the boys chose Pamela. This was a kind of embracing situation, I'd never kissed a girl before, didn't know how to do it and especially didn't want to give it a go. My immediate family weren't affectionate, they never cuddled or kissed me. I had nothing against kissing Pamela, all the boys in the class would have loved to be in my position. We just stood looking at each other in the hall, I didn't know what to say, it felt like a lifetime, then I came up with a plan.

"Just say I kissed you, nobody will know."

Pamela just started laughing, I felt really embarrassed. We returned to the living room and nobody was any the wiser. I got heckled by some of the boys as to how it went in the hall, Brian Hogg wanted to know all the gory details.

"Ye were in there for some time, Raymond."

"No' that long."

The party was a success, there was no fighting, we all had a great laugh. Gerry was the only person in my class who ever invited me to his parties. If truth be told, I can only ever remember getting invited to Gerry's parties at primary school.

The teacher told me to go to the janitor's office during class one day. When I arrived at the office, Kevin and Michael Boyle were there waiting for me. Kevin informed me that Michael picked the school football team. It was common knowledge that it was Primary 7 pupils that made up the team, Primary 6 if you were good enough. I was in Primary 4 and Kevin was telling Michael Boyle I was good enough to make the school team.

"Do you think he's ready, Kevin?"

"Aye, Michael, he scores goals."

Kevin was the captain of the school team; he'd played for the school since Primary 5.

"Okay, Kevin, we'll give him a trial."

They weren't the only trials I had on my mind. I would walk along the top road to Pat Garrity's house on the top road. I would meet up with Pope Garrity and Alan Meharry. We walked across the bing to Tranent for trials with Tranent Legion U10s. The coaches would split us into two groups. There was this guy, Jim Woods, desperate to be the goalkeeper, but he was on the opposing team and I just kept pumping the goals in. He was threatening me with violence, but I just couldn't help but score. I really wanted Jim to be on the team, not that I felt threatened in any way, we had been talking before training and he seemed like a nice guy. He wasn't as happy after training. I got told to bring my football boots at the weekend, he never. As I walked along the dark lane outside the school, I felt my hair getting dragged back. I managed to grab hold of my assailant, a brutal struggle ensued at an acute angle 'til we both met the ground. I managed to get on top and let go a few punches before standing up stamping on his head against the edge of the path, it was big Jim Woods. Pope shouted to me, "Rainbow! C'mon! There's loads of them."

Pope had recognized there was a mob in the lane behind us and just wanted me to walk away. It never stopped us from going to training, it never stopped us from playing for Tranent Legion.

I took my football boots to school for the trial, I was buzzing, all exited, I could hardly concentrate on my work. I kept looking at the boots, I could picture myself scoring the winning goal, it was constantly on my mind. I was in no rush to beat Gerry O'Brian to the front of the class that day, I had other things on my mind. This was my big chance to pull on a Celtic strip, a real one this time, not one of the Thursday market job ones I'd been getting from Roseanne and Eddie every year. Michael Boyle came in the classroom to ask the teacher for permission to trial for the school football team. I was elated, almost jumping out my seat. All the class knew why Michael was here, everyone was looking at me, I just wanted to go and score goals. There was a hush in the room when Miss Thane began to speak.

"Raymond! I'm sorry, I can't allow you to go for the trial because you were off school yesterday."

My heart sank, my head dropped, the laces I was gripping so tightly slipped through my hand like butter melting. I could have been the youngest player ever to play for the school team, Kevin never played 'til he was in Primary 5 and he'd told me he was going to play for Celtic one day. I was gutted, frustrated, angry, all I wanted was a chance. It reminded me of getting let down going to boxing – loving it and that chance being took away like two shakes of a lamb's tale. I sat there reminiscing my short life to date, it was jam-packed with let downs, this was this to become the trend of my life, was I ever going to get a break? Why me! I was told by my parents to stay off school the day before. Michael Boyle looked up at me. "Your day will come, son."

Michael and Kevin had believed in me, I'm sure my classmates also believed. This was a big blow, I never went around to watch the trials at break time, I was too gutted. This wasn't going to get me down for long, every time I got put down, I always seemed to bounce back bigger and stronger.

Ants had devised this game for all the boys to play at dinnertime. It was quite simple really, all you had to do was take turns in sticking the head on your opponent until one gave up. I had worked my way through to the final, it was just Ants and I left. Ants was stubborn, he had a head like concrete, something told me he had played this game many times before. We just stood at the boy's entrance door taking turns to crack the nut on each other. It started off with small headbutts and gradually got harder. Ants wasn't really a fighter, but he had a solid head and he was game as a trout. Something had to give, some boys were shouting, "That's enough!"

This didn't deter Ants, he was giving as good as he got for a wee while at least, then I went in for the kill. I could see his face turn a lighter shade than grey and his eyes were all over the place. Ants never lasted much longer; he was out on his feet.

"That's enough, Rainbow!"

That was the first time I'd played that game; it was a good laugh at the time. I consoled Ants with a cuddle and told him he was a worthy opponent, nobody ever wanted to play that game again.

Everyone in the class gathered at the chapel next to the school, we were making our first communion. We had to enter a small door around halfway down one side to repent our sins, nobody knew what to say. I entered this booth without a clue. The priest was behind a small curtain, he asked me to repeat what he said, then it came to the crunch, for the life of me I couldn't think straight.

"Swearing."

"Ten Hail Marys and our father, my son."

I took a seat near the end of an isle and recited my penance over in my head. Now it was time to receive the body of Christ. We stood in line and worked our way down to the priest.

"Amen."

The priest placed a circular disc on your tongue, you blessed yourself, and returned to your seat, knelt down and quietly said a prayer. The body of Christ could only be described as a flying saucer without the sherbet, I think the proper term for it was rice paper. This was much better than sitting in a classroom trying to beat Gerry to the front of the class. I enjoyed the whole experience that much I became an altar boy. There were three masses on a Sunday, 9am, 11am and 6pm, so I could only manage 6pm, seeing as I was playing football for Tranent Legion on a Sunday. The older boys first gave me a shot of the bells, but I would not stop ringing them when the priest raised his hands, I had to be restrained, I just went wild with the bells. My niche became water and wine which also included holding a silver plate under the recipient's chin during communion. Over your clothes you had to wear a cassock, it was white and covered your body, all my aunties and uncles said I looked like an angel as my hair was pure white. Every Sunday after football I'd go to mass and don the robes without fail, I had a perfect attendance rate at chapel, a lot more than could have been said about the school, belting me every day and making me write lines about the politically correct human being I should become.

We were still going down to Pamela's to play, she was a great laugh. At the side of the houses where she lived there was these doors you could open, essentially, they were coal sellers. This guy came from nowhere.

"What the fuck are you cunts doing?"

I had to step forward and address this person. "Who the fuck are you?"

"Am Tattie Hanratty, the hardest cunt about here."

I punched Tattie into the coal seller, rolled him around and battered him to the ground, Pamela begged me to stop. "You're not the hardest cunt now, pal."

He had both hands covering his head, lying there all curled up. That was the last time he came near us, that was the last time I ever saw him for a very long time.

At school I was mostly fighting everyone else's battles, done it since I got back the use of my legs. I had just got accustomed to it.

Chapter 6

The World Cup 1974 was held in West Germany, it was the first time I'd watched anything on telly apart from boxing. After watching Scotland win 2-0 against Zaire, I was elated. There was World Cup fever in the streets, everyone thought we were going to win the cup. Our neighbors, England, weren't in the competition because they failed to qualify, it was a big deal if you were Scottish. Next up were reigning world champions, Brazil, we got a draw, I was gutted not to see Pelé play, he had retired from international duty. Another draw against Yugoslavia meant we were the only unbeaten team in the competition that year, even though we never qualified from the group stages.

Nancy Clark was always having parties in Fenian Alley when her dad was out drinking. I was the only person not allowed in. I don't know what I had done, Kevin, James and Ricky were all allowed entry, it was not even a goodbye for me, the door just got discreetly closed in my face.

Around Christmas time you could make slides down a hill and do a wee man for as long as you could with a pair of old shoes. This meant starting your run then crouching down like a skier to see who went the furthest.

I hated Christmas, it reminded me of that final onslaught on Boxing Day that led to me being incarcerated in two hospitals. It was getting more predictable each year. Another pair of moccasins from John, £5 from Maria, another Thursday market job Celtic strip and a Celtic football annual from Eddie and Roseanne.

We never had a Christmas tree growing up, it was very informal, more or less, it was just like another day, there were crosses on the wall, but they stayed there all year round. You'd sit with a newspaper on your knees with a plate of stew, we got that every day of the week, Roseanne would always throw in a couple of puff pastries at Christmas. After dinner the cigarettes and pipes would come out, clouds of smoke would fill the air, within seconds the living room was consumed by smoke, I could hardly breath. I hated the smell of smoke, yet this vile toxin was filling my young lungs like pouring water into a kettle.

I hated every minute of that time of year, it just took me back to that helpless wee boy who did nothing wrong, I wasn't that wee boy anymore, I could stick up for myself, I could fight my own battles, it wouldn't happen now. That almost fatal day was engrained in my head forever, Christmas would never be the same again, not that I had a lot to go on since I was so young. I couldn't quite figure it out why it happened to me, and why I never had a mum or dad.

At New year I'd go around to Auntie Anna's, I fancied myself as a bit of a singer. The mike was a beer bottle that got passed around. Kevin was always trying to *free old Wexford town*, I sang 'The Flower of Scotland' – that was my signature song. Alfie would turn his bonnet around and do impressions of Norman Wisdom, he was really funny. I enjoyed New Year at Anna's, it took my mind of what was going through my head for a short time, everyone was so nice – very drunk but nice. I always felt welcome in that house.

My cousin, Victor, would come around on New Year's Day to sing Eddie Irish rebels songs, this was to become a tradition, Eddie loved it.

New Year had gone in a flash, playing football on icy pitches was murder, I never had any shin pads. I always wanted a pair from Tommy Morgan's sports shop. I liked going into Tommy's shop just to look at all the sports equipment I'd buy if I was wealthy.

Getting the belt everyday was the norm since I started school. My hands were freezing from the cold, wearing shorts everyday didn't help, and I'd been walking to and from school since Primary 1, apart from a short stint in a go-kart. I was glad to make it to March, I got the same as usual, a card from John, Maria, and always a special one from Eddie and Roseanne. I wanted a Subbuteo pitch, players, a set of goals and a ball. Roseanne and

Eddie gave me enough money to buy a set of goals and the ball, I used John's spanners, screwdrivers and magnets as my players, the pitch was the bath mattress. I'd spend hours in there, the screwdrivers were the best players. There was a yellow screwdriver, I called it Kenny Dalglish, it could score from anywhere. I was in there for that long Eddie had to go out the back door to do the toilet. These were my only toys, they took me away from the madness, they took me to a happy place, and the bathroom was smoke-free, that was a bonus. But when I was in the house, I always sat across from Roseanne, next to John, Eddie always sat on the other single chair at the window. My young growing lungs were taking a battering with nicotine and all the chemicals that came with the heavy-duty smoke that filled the room.

George, Mamie, Lackie and Agnes would come around for a party from time to time, John would change the records, he was like the DJ. Roseanne would only drink advocaat, it was alcoholic, Eddie and the rest of them would get steaming. I would crawl under the table and cuddle Rover. Eddie kept slapping Rover on the beak. "I'm the master."

Roseanne would tell him to stop, but he kept doing it when he had a good drink in him. These parties would go on 'til late, way past my bedtime. To think, it's the only time Roseanne would let me stay up late enough to watch Monty Python's *Flying Circus* but the telly had been switched off hours ago.

Kevin asked me to join Mickey Conahan's five-a-side team for the civic week. He explained, Mickey was in P7, Kevin and Paul Smith were in P6, Kenny O'Brian was P5, and they wanted me to be their P4, the youngest in the team and they had secured the Celtic strips. It was a no-brainer; Kevin was the best football player in the school.

It was a good feeling pulling on a real Celtic strip. I played up front, where Kevin had intended me to play for the school team, Kevin and Paul played midfield, Mickey was the defender and Kenny played in goals. Kevin and I were banging in the goals as we made our way through the tournament. We played Davie Fisher's team who were in Rangers strips, we annihilated them. We were going from pitch-to-pitch battering goals past every team that played us 'til we finally made it to the final on the best pitch. A grass embankment separated the pitch from the high school tennis courts. The ground was nice and level, nothing like the other pitches that were primarily used for playing rugby.

Before the game we were standing on the Middleshot Square side of the high school, at the gate. I was fast and had almost run myself to a standstill getting to the final, my legs were seizing up. *Just one last effort* – that was going through my mind as I stretched my legs. Kevin told me to be ready and not to sit down or my legs would get cramp. We finally made our way onto the pitch, same formation. It felt like they made this game longer in minutes, we were winning, everyone was playing a blinder. I scored goals, I was a poacher, I was a sprinter but in the second half my legs were giving in, cramping up like you wouldn't believe. I had to signal Kevin, he told me to take the yellow goalies top off Kenny. I had never played in goals in my life, but I could not run anymore. The final whistle blew, Paul told me we had just become the first Catholic side to win the civic week football tournament for primary schools in PrestonPans. It was a prestigious tournament that every kid wanted to win.

We all got presented silver trophies that had a raised black platform. The crowd consumed us as we walked from the pitch all the way up to Preston Road to the foot of Fenian Alley where I went into my Auntie Agnes' house to celebrate. Auntie Agnes filled my cup with Babycham – it was a low alcohol sparkling clear drink, we just had to kid on it was champagne. Agnes took my picture holding the cup high in the air with two hands, I had a smile as wide as the Clyde. Fenian Alley was bouncing that night.

This was a major milestone in my life. When I was in hospital, the doctors told me I may never walk properly again, in the years that followed I had proved them wrong.

Chapter 7

Black bin liners full of clothes started to pile in. There was always lots of jersey and shirts I fancied, sometimes the arms were too long, sometimes the body was too long, it could work both ways, you always found something you could live with, it was great fun.

I served on the alter that Sunday with Paul Cook, we had been doing it every Sunday since we made our first communion. After Mass, my Uncle Jimmy said I looked like an angel and slipped me a ten-pound note.

I still remember the time when Celtic Football Club had the Scottish Cup on display. I got my photo taken with both hands holding the trophy.

We felt like kings walking into St Gabriel's summer fair that year. Everyone knew we had achieved something special, someone bough me a raffle ticket. The summer fair was still a big deal with the locals. I managed to obtain a black jumper with three white stars from the bin liners, it belonged to Victor, I'd had my eye on it for years. It was only a matter of time before it made the rounds. It was a bit long on the sleeves, a couple of turns on the wrists and you were in business. I won a bottle of González Byass, it was a Spanish sherry. Roseanne tried to take it off me, but I was not parting with it. I told her it would be my New Year's bottle, she agreed, and the deal was done.

Eddie and Roseanne took me to Butlin's in Ayrshire. We went down Electric Brae, the driver freewheeled downhill, you were meant to feel like you were going back uphill. Everyone was shouting and screaming, I didn't know what all the fuss was about. We all got our passes for the theme park and dinner hall. Three meals a day and a chalet by the sea, not too bad. I joined a class playing football every day. Eddie bought me a tartan golf hat, I only took that off at night. I slept with my pass around my neck. I tried my hand at roller skating. A guy from Prestonpans called Tommy Garrity – Pope's big brother – he gave me a few tips and in no time I was flying round like John Curry, who won Olympic gold medal at ice skating. I sometimes had to stand outside the Beachcomber while Eddie had a pint. Sometimes I had to go looking for him. It was like a tropical paradise with exotic plants and palm trees. Sometimes I got escorted back to the door for being underage. Nana took me down the beach one day, I got sunstroke. Itching my back off the wall all night, I was exhausted and mentally drained. Apart from that, it was a good holiday, but I was glad to get back to Prestonpans on the east coast.

Port Seton open air swimming pool was now being locally known as the pond. It was something to do in the summer. I enjoyed swimming; I enjoyed the Italian ice cream from the small shop on the corner. The bus fare paid for ice cream, the long walks back and for were like mini adventures.

After the summer holidays, our next teacher was Miss Rushford. I was still getting the belt every day, but it didn't seem to faze this teacher as much as any other I'd previously had. Every report card I'd received read 'too easily distracted, distracts others'. I couldn't see that changing in the foreseeable future.

Sparky regularly came to my house after school. We came home one day and Nana said Rover was dead. Apparently, he'd been run over by a white van at the bottom of the road. I was distraught. Sparky was laughing so I laid him out with a punch. He got showered with apples and bananas by Roseanne to make up for my temper. This was a big deal; Rover was always at the gate waiting for me.

My attendance was much better that year, I got picked to play for the school team. Michael Boyle reminded me, "This is your day, son."

I was the only Primary 5 pupil to play for the school team that year, last year's debacle was paling into a far distant memory now that I was going to be pulling on the green and white hoops. Kevin had first played for the school in Primary 5.

That was good enough for me, considering he wanted to play for his heroes, Celtic. I still had a burning ambition to be a boxer just like my hero Ken Buchanan.

I played center forward for the school team, it was the same position I played for Tranent Legion. Every school we played, no matter what the score, I always scored at least one goal. We played the Protestants at their patch. They were playing in Holland strips; we were donning the green and white hoops of Celtic. There was this huge guy, Harker, shouting his mouth off at us right before kickoff, roaring his lungs out. "GO HOME, YA DIRTY FENIAN BASTARDS!"

The referee said nothing. Big Harker was the bully of the school, and the loudest by the sounds of things. It turned out Harker played at the back and was marking me. All throughout the game Harker was screaming, "FENIAN BASTARDS!"

Kevin ran a through ball for me to chase, I just beat the goalie to it and toe-poked the ball passed him. Harker came flying in from the side and almost broke my leg. I still managed a wee smile as the ball trundled into the net. He should have been sent off for that malicious tackle, he never got a card or a caution. Dragging myself off the ground, I raised both arms in the air as if I was Kenny Dalglish scoring the winning goal in the World Cup. We got slaughtered, but scoring that goal made me feel like a winner.

Roseanne gave me enough money to buy a vinyl 45 single record. I went straight down the bottom Pans and bought Blondie's 'Heart of Glass'. It was the first record I'd ever bought, I cherished it, played Blondie every night.

Chapter 8

There were only two or three chalets booked at Butlin's. You'd think the whole McGuire clan had descended on Ayrshire. Every night I had to sleep on the hard floor with the room smelling of cigarettes and alcohol. My cousin, Pat, from Glasgow, and I would roam the park every day. I was speaking Glaswegian in no time; you tend to pick up accents easily at a young age. Every night there were parties. We were hanging around the grass down from the Beach Ballroom one day, there was races going on. I won the sprint. This girl with grey bell-bottoms picked me as her partner for the wheelbarrow race. I told her to hold on to my legs as tight as possible and run as fast as she could. My arms went as fast as Johnny Weissmuller, who played Tarzan. We won by a country mile. The next up was the three-legged race. You had to tie a piece of cloth around each other's lead foot and run in tandem, we had to practice. I kept my rhythm going with hers 'til I had to drag her over the finish line. Pat never won a race in his age group, so we agreed not to talk about it, within no time I'd forgotten it even happened.

The clan were congregated upstairs in the Beach Ballroom at the back near the fruit machines. Pat was chatting to lassies at the fire escape, he had the gift of the gab. Between chatting to lassies and chasing them, we ended up at the front on the Beach Ballroom where I accidentally nudged into someone. This woman slapped me on the face. We went back to the clan, told Eddie and Uncle Pat. Maria made a mad dash down the front, saying, "Point her out."

"That's her there."

She struck the woman on the face, it turned into a war. It was like the Battle of Bannockburn. We almost got thrown out of Butlin's.

We had a relatively quiet last day in the bottom of the Beach Ballroom. They were handing out prizes.

"Raymond Fraser!"

I was a bit shocked myself, but the clan were even more inquisitive. They presented me with a medal for winning the sprint, just hung it around my neck. I'd won every race that day, so I was up another two times. That night, Pat and I waited on everyone leaving the Beachcomber and heading to this thing called a Chinese takeaway. The smell was lovely, I asked Maria if I could try a bit, but she was parting with nothing. That night the room stunk of sweet Chinese, cigarettes and alcohol. In the morning it was a mad dash to get out in time. The clan made their way back to Glasgow, Fife and Prestonpans. I was glad to get home to sleep in my own single bed, but I missed my cousin, Pat.

I was bouncing about in front of the boys in Kevin's front garden, proudly declaring I could beat Ken Buchanan at the top of my voice. Jamie and Kevin said I couldn't beat big Harker. I disputed that so they arranged a fight after school at the gates of the Protestant school.

Harker looked me up and down as if I was a bit of shite. It was like David and Goliath considering the height and size.

"Come on, ya cunt, hit me!"

"You start it."

Harker shoved me, I shoved him back, then pounced, strangling him to the ground. I could feel my arm tightening around his neck.

"Let me go!"

Jamie and Kevin both intervened.

"Do you give up?"

"Aye!"

I gently released my grip; he was gulping for air. I stood and looked down at him holding his throat. After that day, all the Catholics walked home with me past the Protestant school.

Mark and I were playing two drunks in the school play. This was my first leading role on the stage. Miss Rushford half-filled two bottles of whiskey with cold tea to give it a dramatic affect. On cue, we staggered to the front of the stage pretending to be drunk while singing 'I Belong to Glasgow', only stopping to take a swig from the bottle. It tasted horrible though I was more determined to pull it off. I sang the first verse, Mark was to sing the second verse, but he was stuttering, totally forgot his lines so I carried on singing his verse. We ended up getting a standing ovation, I'd never been drunk in my life.

I dreaded Christmas coming, especially Boxing Day. There were no apparent surprises. Moccasins from John, £5 from Maria, Celtic annual and market job Celtic strip from Roseanne and Eddie. I also got a card with each present, Roseanne and Eddie always put kisses. I never physically got the kisses, not never, they were old-school. There was still no sign of a Christmas tree or decorations. We had stew, tatties and puff pastries, just like any other week.

That New Year I got hammered on the González Byass sherry I'd won at the summer fair. After Lackie, Agnes, George and Mamie arrived, I kept nipping through to the wardrobe where Eddie kept his drink. John was always the resident DJ at a house party – earphones, the lot. You'd think he had a set of decks he took it that seriously. Pat McCue would come in, dropping ash all over the floor from his cigarette, singing, 'I'm Nobody's Child' in the style of Billy Connelly. I totally underestimated the strength of the sherry. One minute I was rocking out to 'Sgt Pepper's Lonely Hearts Club Band', the next thing I was on the deck, splitting my head off the coffee table. It was an early bed for the lad that night.

Violently sick through the night, like a bear with a sore head in the morning. It wasn't worth it; I could live without another drink in my life. I lay on the couch moaning; the symptoms were getting worse as the day unfolded. There's no way I could put myself through that again. I was drinking too fast, too young, to understand the consequences, Roseanne and Eddie had no sympathy for me.

"You'll no' do that again, lad."

Eddie never spoke much unless he had a drink in him, but he always told the truth.

"No chance."

Back at school, I told my mates about the New Year scenario involving the sherry and coffee table. Ants was pissing himself, he claimed to have smoked a cigar. I hated the smell of smoke, especially cigarettes and pipe. That concoction was driving me off my nut. Ants claimed to have done a lot of things, I believed him about the cigar. It wasn't long 'til I was banging in a solitary goal for the school team on the receiving end of a hammering. Just pulling on the hooped jersey made the hairs on the back of my neck stand up. It was the last year St Gabriel's were to play in Celtic strips.

My birthday came again, I was 10 years old. I got the usual cards from John and Maria. Roseanne and Eddie would always get me a wee treat, there was always lots of kisses on their card. They never actually gave me any kisses for real, they were not affectionate in the slightest, by any stretch of the imagination. It was something I couldn't understand, I couldn't put my finger on it. I'd saw the way my friends were with their parents; it wasn't the same in our house.

I wrote a letter to an entertainment show called *Jim'll Fix It*, it was presented by Jimmy Saville. He made dreams come true for kids, I watched it all the time. I wanted to fight Ken Buchanan in a boxing ring, that was my dream as a kid, it was my ambition in life. I wrote a letter and gave it to Roseanne to post for me. Thank fuck he never got back to me; Saville might have got me in the ring.

Our teacher asked us to learn a Robert Burns poem. It was for a show where you had to go on stage and read your poem in front of the whole school to achieve a certificate.

In preparation we had to practice in front of our class. Everyone was just like reading the poem of their choice. I dramatically enacted the recital using every inch of my body and every scale of my lungs. The class were screaming with laughter, the teacher said I was excellent.

On the day of the poem contest, I brought the house down with my rendition of *To a Mouse*. Everyone in the hall congratulated me. I felt proud of my performance. This was the first time I had really shown what I could do, it was such a powerful burst of exhilaration. Just as satisfying as winning Prestonpans' five-a-side tournament.

I went to a kids disco in the British Legion with Dukey and Paul McGuire. There was this one girl I was immediately attracted to. I tried my best not to let her see I was admiring her by looking away anytime we got close to eye contact. She was beautiful, it was really hard to avoid her. I wasn't a dancer, so I was caught between a rock and a hard place. We were all sitting around the table, she was chatting to people then swapping seats getting closer. She was always laughing and could talk for Scotland. I was starting to panic seeing as I was really shy around girls and not much of a talker. She finally made her way over to me, talking that fast I could hardly keep up with her.

We spoke for ages just like I'd known her for years. Outlandishly forward thinking she struck a chord with me that I would never forget. She said she wanted to be my first. By first, she meant the first person to sleep with me when we had grown up. The conversations got so heated I could have done with a cold shower. I tried to laugh it off, but she insisted she wanted to be my first. She instantly became my childhood sweetheart; I'd never met a girl like her before. We'd barely met but vowed a solemn promise. I didn't know where my head was at that day, we were just two kids who were love-struck. I thought about her for a while after, I never forgot that day or the promise. She told me her name was Dot.

Chapter 9

Apparently, my wild streak was rubbing off on Tombo, according to his parents who sent a letter to our teacher forbidding him to play with me. They had pleaded with the teacher to keep us apart. We weren't allowed to play at school or after. I had to meet him in secret, bribe his sister when required.

I was hanging about a lot with Pope and Alan Meharry doing the Grand National jumping and climbing over fences and hedges all the way down the back gardens of Preston Terrace. When we ran out of competitors, who had either been injured or caught by the tenants, the three of us would play catch help, we'd play for hours. When I was doing the catching, Pope and Alan started shouting, "C'mon, Cannon!"

My nickname was Rainbow, so I was wondering why they were calling me Cannon. "What de ye mean Cannon? "

"Never mind! C'mon, Cannon!"

It went on like that for ages. They had always called me Rainbow, everyone called me Rainbow, how did I suddenly get this new nickname? The only Cannon I'd ever heard about was the one o'clock gun at Edinburgh Castle. It mystified me; I was intrigued why they called me that name. No matter how many times I asked, they refused to tell me. I felt a bit strange walking along Gardiner Terrace at the top of the Pans then cutting down into my street. My nickname was always Rainbow.

It was just a normal day playing catch help with Pope and Alan but there was something strange about it. I couldn't quite get my head around the name; they wouldn't tell me why. When I got home, I asked Roseanne why I was getting called Cannon. When my eyes started to narrow, Roseanne always knew I was deep in thought.

"Sit down, son." She burst into tears and came back holding a piece of paper. "If you could pick any dad in the world, who would it be?"

"I don't know what you mean."

"Pick anyone in the world, who would you like your dad to be?"

"That's easy, ma hero, Ken Buchanan"

"He's your real father, son."

"Aye, get away!"

"Honestly, son"

I thought she was winding me up. I'd not long wrote away to *Jim'll Fix it* to fight Ken Buchanan, that was my lifetime ambition.

"No way, he can't be my dad."

"He's your real dad, son."

"You're at the wind up?"

"Who do you think your mother is?"

"Not got a clue."

She showed me this piece of paper and said, "This is your birth certificate."

I never knew what a birth certificate was, I was only 10, I'd never seen a one before in my life. "Kenneth Buchanan, who's that?"

"That's your dad, son, he gets called Ken."

"Aye, right! It says he's a joiner/carpenter. In 1966 Ken Buchanan was a professional boxer."

"We had to put that down in case you found out. Look at who your real mother is, son"

"Mary Fraser? Did you have a sister that died?"

"No, son, Mary Fraser is Maria Fraser. She preferred being called Maria."

"No way, I always thought she was my sister."

"No, son, she's your real mother, she should have told about this a long time ago, but you know now."

"So John's not my brother?"

"He's your real uncle, son."

"What about Alan and Linda?"

"They're your brother and sister."

"So, what about you and Eddie?"

"We're your real granny and grandad, son."

The saying goes, success has many fathers, but failure is an orphan, in many ways, I was like an orphan, destined to fail.

In one day, I found out my hero was my real dad, my mother was my sister, my brother was my uncle, my niece and nephew were my brother and sister, and who I regarded as my mum and dad were my real granny and grandad. This was a lot to take in, I didn't want to believe this could be happening to me. Why me! After everything that happened in my childhood, why this! Who in the world could begin to imagine that their lifelong hero was their real dad, it was unbelievable how everyone could have kept this a secret. Why would you do such a horrible thing? It was nothing short of miraculous how I made it through the early years. The delusion of having or belonging to any pure substance began to escape the logic of my existence. Everything in my life seemed to be going one hundred miles an hour. I hadn't time to think about my life to date, I hadn't time to think about much apart from getting through it, one day at a time. I've spent too much time chasing shadows. It's all been a deluded illusion of integrity that I'd fallen for most of my natural life. No more games, no more lies and deceit. I was a tough kid, but my head felt like it was discombobulated. I always thought it was strange that all my friends had mums and dads, even grannies and grandads.

"Why did you no' tell me?"

"We couldn't, son, that was up to Maria. Look, son, you can go to the authorities about this, but you'll just get taken off us."

I didn't know what the authorities was, and I didn't want to get taken off Eddie and Roseanne. I always wondered why I was fighting every day.

Everyone in Prestonpans must have knew who I was except me. Did they want to fight me because I was Ken Buchanan's son? I reckoned that would be an accolade for beating me. But nobody ever beat me since I was abused as a child. Lots of strange innuendoes went through my mind like a wildfire of discontent and injustice. *Why is this happening to me?* went over and over in my head 'til I felt sick. I was always the odd one out, even as a child they dressed me as an Indian when every other boy in the street was a cowboy with guns and holsters, I wanted to be a cowboy. I always wanted a mum and dad. I wrote a letter to Santa every year asking for a mum and dad. What was I going to do now? I'd never cried in my life except when I got abused. I was a love child that went wrong, a Fenians bastard. All I ever wanted was to be was normal. In a weird kind of fashion, I was the only normal one out the lot of them.

My life up until this point was like a nightmare followed by horrible dream. I was a boxer, I was a football player, nobody could beat me at school sports, nobody could beat me at fighting. It wasn't enough, it wasn't good enough to be told the truth. If I had my dad when I was a child, he would have knocked the shit out of anyone trying to abuse me. Eddie was a quiet man; he never laid a finger on me. When he came home from work, he gave Nana a piece of his mind. He was my best pal, he never said much but that night they almost got in a fight.

"He should have been told, it's your fault. I told you!" Eddie kept saying it over and over. His face was red and angry. It was the most I'd heard him talk and he just kept on repeating himself.

I went to bed with a heavy heart that night. I was so confused, mystified and bewildered. I loved Eddie and Nana. I didn't want the authorities to know because Nana said I'd be taken away.

Roseanne told me they had to stop me going to boxing when I was eight because they didn't want me to turn out like my real dad. I loved boxing and I was good at it. I wanted to be like Ken Buchanan, my real dad. It was the one thing I always wanted to do, now she was saying I could go when I had left the school and had a job. It just seemed to be one lie after another. I had played football since I was seven, but I always wanted to be a boxer. I was angry that they took me away from boxing, but I also liked playing football.

They had tried their best to hide the truth. Were they ever going to tell me? That was the question playing on my mind.

That Sunday, when Maria came down to visit with Alan and Linda, I made sure I never went out with my pals. When Alan and Linda were playing out the back garden, I confronted Maria at the living room door. "Are you my ma?"

She looked over at Roseanne and said, "Have you been talking to him?"

"Aye! He knows, you should have told him a long time ago."

Maria said she would talk to me about it one night at her house when Tom was out.

Chapter 10

Maria took me to her house with Alan and Linda. It was all nice and cozy, lovey-dovey to start with. Linda cuddled up to me on one chair, Alan sat on another, Maria on the couch spouting out how we were not to treat each other as half-brother and sister, but full brother and sister. She suddenly spouted lucidly that I would not be left nothing if anything happened, her words were made clear and concise that night. As a family, it would be down to Allan and Linda to decide if I got anything from their family estate. Off course, they both agreed to make sure everything would be equal. I was ten years old; Alan was six, Linda was four. I never really thought that much about it at the time. Didn't really understand what she was directly expressing at the time. I was so young, confused about in many ways.

Why was she telling a young boy such a mature theme? The predominant matters discussed that night stayed with me forever.

There was nothing equal about us. They lived in a big fancy house; Alan's bedroom was half the size of my house that lay on a council estate in Prestonpans. A blind man could see there was no equality. I only had an old bed in a corner of a small room I shared with John, who literally took up 95% of it. That was the very first comparison that hit me. I would have loved to have my own bedroom, anything, no matter what size it was. Anything to get away from the thick, wretched smell of smoke that continually filled the air and stayed there all night and day. The small bathroom was my reprieve.

Anytime I brought anything up with Maria, she would always come back with, "What about all the starving bairns in Africa?"

I just had to get on with things. Take everyone at face value, take everyone for their word. The visiting scenario was a bit of a dampener.

I sat down with Roseanne and Eddie. To make them sound younger, I decided to call them Rose and Ed. That was their new, revised names. It's all I could think about doing under the circumstances.

It was the day of the all-star charity football match. Rose and Ed gave me enough money for bus fairs and enough to buy a program. They told me to stick with the oldest boy – that was Paul Mulgrew. Kev, Jamie, Ricky, Archie, quite a few boys came along. We got on the bus to Edinburgh arriving early at Meadowbank Stadium. We took our seats in the stand, it was a great day for a game of football. My dad was playing on the right wing for Radio Forth. Jim Watt was meant to be playing for Radio Clyde, but he didn't show up.

I can't remember the score but Radio Forth won the game. And my dad played a blinder on the wing.

After the game, hordes of fans were gathering at the end of the wall that separated the crowd from the player's tunnel. Everyone wanted Ken Buchanan's autograph. We had to patiently wait till the crowd grew smaller and smaller. I was almost there; I was so nervous and exited at the same time. Ken Buchanan was my favorite boxer on the telly since I was three years old. Now I was almost within touching distance of the man who was my hero and real dad. Kevin and Jamie were pushing me in the back, telling me to shout 'Dad', but I was too scared to do it. I'd only seen him on the telly, now I was handing him my programme to sign with. I said, "Thank you!" I started to look for Paul Mulgrew while having one last look at my hero.

Paul said we had to leave now if we were going to make the bus, I left immediately with Paul – they were my instructions from Nana and Eddie. The rest of the boys stayed behind. Kevin and Jamie said to my dad that his son was here, he'd just got an autograph from him. He asked where I was. The boys had a look for me, but I was long gone. They told me he stayed back a while and had a blether with them. I was gutted, I could hardly get the words out my mouth to ask him to sign my programme but to have a chat would have been fantastic. From the moment I saw him glide across the boxing ring to the day I found out he was my dad, I worshiped him like a king. He was a god in my eyes. To think I could have actually spoken to him if I'd stayed back. He told Kevin and Jamie he wanted to speak to me.

I really wanted to meet my dad, Rose and Ed said it would take time because he has another family. But within a few weeks, he'd made contact with Maria and a date had been set. I couldn't wait, it seemed like a lifetime but before you knew it, I was playing on the grass opposite my house when this big grey Daimler car drove down the street, the registration on the car read KB 123. I walked over to the house, he was already inside.

"All right, son?"

"Aye."

I was too shy to talk, I was awestruck, I couldn't believe my dad had come to see me. It felt like a dream, but it was real. Ken Buchanan, my hero, my dad, was standing in our living room. We went outside and Nana took a photo. He was wearing white shoes, white trousers and a white T-shirt that had Ken Buchanan Hotel printed on it. He asked if I'd like to go for something to eat up in Edinburgh. I jumped at the chance and said, "Aye."

I think it was the only car parked in the street. There weren't many cars passed our house in those days, money was tight. The car had cream leather seats; the dashboard looked amazing. On our way up town, I hardly uttered two words.

I had all these things I wanted to ask him, but I bottled it up inside. I wanted to know what it was like to be world champion, fight at Madison Square Garden, there was lots of things I wanted to know. I wanted to know why he didn't come to see me when I was a kid, and most of all I wanted to know if I'd see him again.

He took me to this Italian restaurant in the west end of Edinburgh. I hadn't a clue what to pick so he ordered it for me. All I could say was, "Aye."

He told me it was spaghetti carbonara, I just nodded my head. My dad had this round kind of meat with a piece of bone sticking straight out. It looked much better than what I was having. However, I did enjoy what I was given. We also had a pudding, I asked for strawberry ice cream – that was my favorite. Once we had finished, he drove me home. I got out the car and spoke.

"Cheerio, Dad."

"See you again soon, son."

I couldn't believe I'd just called Ken Buchanan 'dad', but it just felt like the natural thing to say. I couldn't believe he'd called me son; I was well proud. I found it very difficult to sleep that night. There were no words I could say that could describe how I was feeling. It was a magical day; one I'd never forget for the rest of my life.

My dad was back the following week. This white Old English sheepdog came bounding in the garden as I waited for my dad, it was so friendly we rolled about the front grass. It was a big dog, it just kept licking me as we tumbled over and over. Then my dad appeared at the front gate.

"Denver!"

The dog backed away ever so slightly so that I could get my arms around his neck and roll him over again. I loved dogs; this was a cracker though. My dad let us play for a while.

"I'll show you my hotel, son."

"I love this dog, dad."

"Aye! He's all right, son."

Chapter 11

Our teacher in Primary 6 was Miss Kieller. She almost broke down with the amount of times she had to give me the belt. The word was going about she was on medication. My classmates kept looking at me in a different light since I found out who my family was, I'm sure they all knew long before I did. I had it in my head everyone in the Pans knew before me. Part of me felt ashamed, part of me felt confused and part of me felt glad I'd found out. My mind was going 100 miles per hour. I was increasing observant to people's reactions. I was now captain of the school team, playing football took my mind off what was going on in my life. Miss Kieller was not sympathetic in any way, she belted me every day. I was the odd one out, this wasn't something new to me. Since I had found out who I was, I trusted no one. I was continually getting asked how my surname was Fraser and my dad's was Buchanan. I lost count of the amount of times I tried my best to explain. I was an outgoing boy who turned into a relatively quiet but angry young boy. I always had a quick temper, this new anger I felt was at life in general.

Miss Keiller told us all about the slavery that still existed in South Africa, everyone in the class thought it was disgusting. Two pupils would be joining us from there, so we were told to be nice to them, she personally asked me to look after them. Michael Mcgoff and Andrew Vidler got announced to the class soon after. Michael stayed up my street, he was a quiet wee guy who kept singing a song about a guy called Daniel Boone. I hit it off straight away with Andrew, we became best friends. He invited me down to his home in Cockenzie for a game of Subbuteo with his big brother. It was only a couple of miles from my house. I met his sisters who were wee drama queens. His sister, Susan, went on to star in *Trainspotting* as the junkie who lost her baby. The games room was in the attic, you had to negotiate a set of steep steps to get there. A full-size pitch was at the far end with actual players, it looked tremendous. I was so quick with my hands I beat Andrew and his brother. I had always wanted to play on a full-size Subbuteo pitch, it was much better than playing on a small bathroom carpet using John's tools. I went away delighted; they were such a nice family.

That Christmas we were invited to Maria's house for dinner. I was told in advance not to mention my dad's name around the table. Their big fancy bought house was in a quiet part of Bonnyrigg. It was a new house; they were still building new houses at the top of the street all next to a private golf course. My now brother and sister had a room each that, combined, was bigger than our house in the Pans, there was even a garage built onto the side of their house. What a Christmas tree they had in the living room; it was outstanding.

I was desperate to mention my dad's name at Christmas dinner but had to bite my tongue. I was glad when the festive season was over. There were no big surprises except for not being able to talk about my dad. Maria's big present was this thing with two handles and three long sets of coiled springs, it was to work your chest. It nearly took the skin off my chest. I never used it again. John got me another set of moccasins, Rose and Ed got me another market job Celtic strip with a lovely card. My dad had bought me a bike, it was a racer, but I wanted an adult one like Jamie and Ricky. I had to compromise so I exchanged it for a chopper, Kevin got a chopper that year also.

Prestonpans WAC were starting to jell quite nicely. We were all getting better at following Gary Fraser's lead vocals in the minibus going to away games. I was amazed how he knew all the words to all of ABBA's greatest hits, he astounded me.

While practicing sprinting with Andrew at school, I always got away to the quickest start, but he eventually caught me most of the time. My unbeaten record at all events in sports day was in jeopardy. I partnered Andrew in the wheelbarrow and three-legged races, the only one I was confident of winning was the obstacle race. When the day came, I got the edge on Andrew with a fast start in the sprint, he came back and pipped me to the post. I was that gutted I gave away my ticket to get sweets. We won the other two races comfortably. He was a big muscly boy who I reckoned would be stiff at obstacle races, I was right, he never made the first three. I didn't know your tickets counted as points this year for a trophy and a medal for sportsman of the year. I'd have won it if I never gave my stint ticket away. A guy in the year above me called Paul Lavin beat my score by two points. I was really angry inside for giving my ticket away, I still congratulated Paul, admired his medal and vowed not to give my ticket away in anger if I got beat next year – I'd only lost by two points.

The football season had finished we didn't win the league or any cups, but it was starting to get promising, so I concentrated on playing golf.

Rose and Ed came to the door to see us off. My dad had a big car. Denver was a big dog, his head was almost between us while my he was driving. My dad took me to a place called Ferry Road in Edinburgh. His hotel looked like a small castle, Buchanan tartan carpets throughout. In the function room there was a boxing ring, he told me that's where the band would play. All the alcoves were filled with iconic framed boxing bills. I played with Denver out the back for ages. He was such a lovely big dog who had a good nature. We rolled about for ages. His coat was so fluffy, he was just like the dog in the Dulux paint advert. We became best friends instantly. I asked my dad why he called him Denver.

"He's named after my favorite singer, John Denver, son."

The hotel chef made me something to eat. My dad said I could have anything I wanted, I just let him choose for me. It was a massive change from Rose's daily watered-down stew. I was handed a plate of tagliatelle; my dad was pasta in the brain. Once again, it was delicious. It was officially my new favorite dish. When I was finished, my dad looked over. "I'll need to take you home, son."

I gave Denver a huge cuddle and let him lick me all over my face. In no time we arrived outside my house.

"See you soon, son."

"See you later, dad."

I really missed playing with Denver, he was a great dog. And I really missed being with my dad.

Chapter 12

It was late one evening when there was a knock at the door. I was in the vicinity, so I answered it – it wasn't like me. There was this small, elderly man with a full head of hair who was well dressed.

"Hello, Raymond."

"Who are you?"

"I'm your grandad. Can I come in?"

I wasn't too sure, so I went to ask Rose. She returned to the living room with the well-dressed man. "This is your grandad, son, he's your dad's dad."

"Aw right!"

Rose went to put the kettle on, I felt kind of comfortable in his company. It wasn't long before I sang to the tune and started calling him grandad. He'd heard I liked sports. I told him I played for Prestonpans WAC, I played center forward and loved scoring goals. I told him I scored a hat-trick in my first game then got sent off for kicking the goalie in the face, but I really wanted to be a boxer when I was older. I told him I'd followed boxing since I was three years old. I'd punch Eddie's hands when my dad was fighting. He told me my dad's trainer was also called Eddie. He asked me if

I'd like to play golf on Sunday morning real early at Portobello Links. It was a 9-hole course, a good place to start, he told me that's where he began playing.

"Av no' got any clubs apart from an auld putter."

"That's okay, Raymond, we can share mine."

I jumped at the chance. He told me we'd tee off at 9am in the morning so I'd be back in time to play football in the afternoon. After his cup of tea, he said he was off. "I just wanted to see you, son."

I ushered him to the door, waving 'till his car was out of sight. Back in the living room, Rose had some explaining to do.

"So that was the well-dressed man who came to visit me in hospital?"

"Yes, son! He'd brought you jumping beans from America."

As promised, Grandad was at my door around 8am on Sunday morning. We drove to Portobello and waited on our tee-off time. I had more than a few practice swings. On the tee I must have swung at least 20 times before I managed to slice the ball into the rough. Apart from the rough, I was in more bunkers than Churchill. I pretty much kept to the rough and bunkers all the way round, occasionally digging uptake fairway. We lost a ton of balls. Eventually I went from slashing the rough to digging up most fairways. I was in bunkers that long I was waiting on someone throwing me a cigar. The only thing I was good at was putting.

Grandad would tally up the scores, I was always miles behind to start with, after a period of time the scores were getting closer. Close enough he bought me a ragtag set of golf clubs and a bag to put them in. None of the clubs were the same make. Like a kind of mongrel assortment of makeshift renegades that I had to discover a way to play every single different club, except the putter, which was my own. The shafts weren't straight, especially the 7 iron. A set of clubs were hard to come by in the 70s, so I felt grateful that grandad had gone to the trouble of buying me them. He had also bought me a brand new trolley that could be used in summer or winter, so it was easier to carry my clubs. That trolley came in mighty handy as I zigzagged my way around the course.

After playing golf, I'd play for Prestonpans WAC, either at home across the road in Polwarth Park or away games in the minibus. We were the only team I'd ever heard of that sang Abba songs. Gary Fraser was the front man; he knew all the words. Captain of the team, the dancing queen. When we all started to lose track of one song, Gary would belt out another.

Granda and I started to squeeze two rounds out of the 9-hole course, I must have been getting better. One day he told me he'd take me to Monktonhall Golf Club. It was an 18-hole coarse in Musselburgh, but I had to plenty trade here at Portobello where he started as a kid. I started to hit most fairways, with the amount of digging I was doing I could have got a part-time job in the graveyard.

In Primary 7, Miss McCann was belting me a multitude of times every day. It got way out of hand it became so embarrassing. Considering the changes in my life, it was lucky I still managed to make it to school at all. I wish we could have got Miss Souter again, she never had the heart to belt me. The teachers must have all known, they all read the newspapers. But I'd got the belt every day since Primary 1. Just for trying to have a laugh, just out of boredom, just for attention. My life was slowly going down the drain. Nothing about me was normal. I was getting the belt that much Rose went around to school and slapped Miss McCann in the face. She was also going to set about the headmaster, Jock Reynolds, I'd never seen that man so humble in all my days. Now I was back to just getting the belt once a day, I didn't feel so bad.

We just got a new headmaster and I'd just kicked a ball through the toilets window. He was definitely out to make a name for himself the way he punished me by lashing my hands along the corridor between two classroom doors. His name was Mr Taylor, he was young, he thought he was a big man behind a length of leather when I couldn't hit him back. I don't know how I managed to keep things together during such an emotional part of my young life. I was captain of the school team again. My five-a-side team made the semifinals of the gala week, we never lost a game, our opponents got a corner in our final game and went through to the final on that account, there were no penalties.

Chapter 13

I really wanted to see this film called *Saturday Night Fever*. I was too young but really liked the music.

My granda told me I was ready to take on Monktonhall golf course in Musselburgh. My God! It was a long course. He took me for an ice cream at St Lucas in Musselburgh after the game. I ordered a knickerbocker Glory, it was amazing. Lucas did the best ice cream on the east coast. The scores we're getting close, so he made an offer that if I beat him, I'd get an ice cream. We shook hands on the deal. He told me in the car, "There's only one thing better than a knickerbocker Glory, that's two knickerbocker Glories."

Occasionally I beat him and my choice of ice cream had changed to a chocolate nut sundae. The agreement gave me the impetus to try even harder.

St Gabriel's Youth Club on a Wednesday night, hanging about with Gerry. We met two older girls, never seen them before. They just started talking to us. I was really shy around girls. There was a movie playing in the room adjacent to the main sports hall. We went in as two couples. After a while, I noticed Gerry putting his arm around his girl, I couldn't summon the courage to do that. When the movie ended, we respectfully walked the girls home in different directions. Agnes lived between the post office and police station, close to where I walked Matty and Sandy to get their bus. We stood there looking at each other. I was so shy, Agnes had to say something.

"Are you not going to kiss me?"

I paused for a moment.

"Well, aye!"

It took great courage to close my eyes, lean forward and touch lips. I hadn't a clue what I was doing. I'd never kissed anyone before in my life. Agnes Burns was the first girl I ever kissed, it was kind of awkward, we fell through the hedge. Then she offered me her paper round. I had to go along with the notion with the knowledge that getting up for school was a tremendous effort. This became the norm on a Wednesday for a wee while until the morning I had arranged to meet her at the bottom pan's newsagents. Of course I never turned up, too tired to go out delivering papers so early in the morning to houses in streets I was not overly familiar with. That's when the kissing stopped. I avoided the Wednesday Club like the plague due to the embarrassment of letting Agnes down.

I pulled the cassock over my clothes, made my way down the corridor with another altar boy.

Suddenly I felt something lodging its way between the cheeks of my bum, then all of a sudden, a sharp jolting poke up my arse by the priest's umbrella.

"C'mon! Move along."

"Fuck off!"

That was the last time I served at mass. There was no way I was going through that ordeal again, I felt violated. The priest had jabbed me up the arse with the mettle point of his black umbrella.

Immersing myself in football helped the mechanism of my brain deal with the constant recurring reminders of being abused.

Maria took me to Bonnyrigg, to visit Alan and Linda. I met up with Russel, we went climbing trees up the golf course with Alan. I was like a monkey swinging from tree to tree. Russel wasn't as confident as me, but he made it up. One big tree Alan wanted to scale with us, so we gave him a hand to get started. With a wee bit of encouragement, he got quite far up the tree. They had to call the fire brigade to get him down. Then I was back down the Pans as quick as you like.

Prestonpans WAC won the Lee Anderson trophy and Longniddry Gala Cup. We beat Tranent in both finals, they were rare and cherished occasions. I played my heart out at Longniddry. Rab Donaldson came over to me, said the boys had been voting for man of the match. He said I could pick myself, he also said it was a draw between Rab Cochrane and I so it was up to me. I knew Rab wouldn't pick himself, so I turned and said, "Rab Cochrane."

I'd regularly got the bus to Musselburgh and walked around a mile up a steep hill to Stoneybank to visit my granda. He told me lots about my dad during my visits. Whilst we were talking, I gathered this information.

My dad got bullied at school. His Auntie Agnes bought him a pair of boxing gloves for Christmas. After my granda took him to watch *The Joe Louis Story* he was hooked. He won his first fight at 3st 2lb, there was no stopping him after that. He had to pass a Catholic school where they would chase him all the way home. He had a glittering amateur career. He also played football for Northfield Boys Club. He became Scottish senior champion but couldn't go to the commonwealth games because he was under the age restriction.

At the tender age of 17, he lost a heavily disputed semifinal decision to double Olympic champion, Stanislav Stepashkin, it was in Berlin behind the Iron Curtain. All the Western press had him winning that fight. He was quickly running out of live opposition so had to do an exhibition with Scotland's Dick McTaggart, who won Olympic gold medal and the Val Baker Award for being the best boxer of the games. My dad won The British ABA title then turned professional. In his first professional fight, he beat Brian Tonks by second round KO. He went on to win the Scottish title. Then he went on to beat Jim 'Spike' McCormack on points to win to win a British title eliminator, which was his hardest fight to date. He beat Maurice Cullen by KO in the 15th round to win the British title.

He signed to fight Ismael Laguna for the undisputed world title. By the time 26th September 1970 came along, the WBC had refused to sanction the fight in San Juan, Puerto Rico. He was only fighting for one version against the undisputed lineal champion. The fight was in an open-air car park, the temperature was 120 degrees in the shade. He won the WBA title on points. He had to go back over to Los Angeles in America to do it all over again, beating Ruben Navarro on points to win the undisputed crown. That reaffirmed him lineal champion since 1970. He was jointly awarded British Sports Personality of The Year with Princess Anne; he graced the dance floor with a princess.

He fought eight times as lineal undisputed world champion, only four were sanctioned. He fought on the same bill as Muhammad Ali twice, once getting the star dressing room where Ali's coach, Angelo Dundee, had to ask my granda if my dad would be okay to let Ali share his dressing room when he fought Canadian champion and 4th ranked welterweight in the world, Donato Paduano. He gave away almost a stone in weight that night.

He was the first British boxer to win the American Sports Writers of the Year Award, only the second person in Europe, Joe Frazier and Muhammad Ali were next on the list – that's some company to keep.

After that low blow defeat to Roberto Duran he came back to Scotland to win the Lord Lonsdale Belt by defeating future world champion, Jim Watt, in Glasgow. His only regret was not fighting in his home city of Edinburgh. He had adopted Madison Square Garden in New York as his home ground fighting many times in America, and all over the world. He must have been one of the most travelled boxers in history. My grandad told me lots about my dad. He did honour his word and gave Laguna a rematch in Madison Square Garden in what turned out to become a bloodbath where his coach nicked his swollen eye with a razor. Duran would never fight him again; he always maintained my dad was his hardest opponent and the best fighter he'd ever fought. In New York, United States of America they called my dad King Kenny.

This was a lot to take in for such a young boy. I knew my dad was a great boxer. The facts only contribute to a testimony that can only be described as 'legend'. Dancing around in those Buchanan tartan shorts all over the world, especially New York City. Topping the bill to a man who was voted Sportsman of the Twentieth Century – none other than Muhammad Ali. And the compliment, 'hands of stone', which Roberto Duran gave him. Muhammad Ali was the greatest of all time, Roberto Duran has to be close. My dad was a boxing legend.

I was breaking records myself without the caliper. Against all the odds, against what my doctors told me, I was an achiever myself. Something that looked out of sight at one point. Remarkably, I'd turned the tables on all medical assessments. I was resilient.

On school sports day I achieved the same as the year before, only losing the sprint. This time, I didn't give my ticket away and won Sportsman of the Year, Pamela's sister, Monica Dixon, won Sportswoman.

At the end of the school year, my dad came to an open day. All the other kids surrounded him. I had said hello when he came in then stood near the other side of the hall, there was a battle going on for his attention. He never stayed long, but I was glad he made an appearance,

I had gone through primary school seeing a speech therapist and I could hardly string a sentence together without swearing.

Chapter 14

The 'fasten your seat belts' sign came on and we were on our way to Benidorm. This was my first time outside Scotland; I was going to make the most of it. Maria kept swapping seats with someone in the smoking area at the back of the plane, she was up and down like a yoyo, I was sitting at the window next to Russell. I don't know why I was sitting at the window because I was scared of heights, looking over the ramparts of Edinburgh Castle was enough for me. The plane hit a lot of turbulence before we landed with more than a few bumps, everyone in the plane started clapping and singing. The drive from the airport to Benidorm was relatively short but we must have gone up and down every wee windy street in the old town of Benidorm by the time we got there.

We finally arrived at our hotel, the pool was small and manky, and there were dead or dying insects all over the surface. Maria, Rose and I were meant to be sharing a room on the third floor but Maria never actually slept there, she was always in Palm and Olive's room.

After dumping the cases, we all went for a walk around the old town of Benidorm, Russell and I bought huge knives that had a stop around your waist and a holster to put them in. The knives were that big you could almost play sword fighting – you'd never get away with that in Scotland. I had my eye on a small gun. Maria almost bought me it until she found out it was actually a real gun. Rose would take Russell and I home as Maria and the women would go to the nightclubs. Maria never returned to the room, it was that hot I never really slept much.

One night we all ended up in in a hotel called Los Pelicanos to watch Spanish dancers. We were in the bar and this guy was all over Maria like a rash.

"Fuck off, ya cunt."

I stood my ground against this man, Nana told me to calm down but there was another guy trying it on with Rose, she'd had a few drinks and was laughing, I punched this guy. For my behavior Rose took Russell and I back to the hotel we stayed in, she said we were too young to watch the dancers. Maria stayed out all night again. Russell ended up taking Maria's bed. We would tap out tunes on each other's head and you had to guess the song.

We went to breakfast one morning and there was a fly in my salad. They brought me another one and there was another fly in it. I hated sunbathing, I was as white as a sheet. I'd cover myself in towels and just lie there boiling. There was no pigment in my skin, I always got burnt, heat rash or sunstroke.

You could find almost anything in Benidorm. One night I got my photo taken holding a tiger. I went up to where Maria was sleeping one morning and there was a guy lying in a bed, I'd never seen him in my life before that morning.

Russell and I were always playing spy games armed with the knives. When Russell grew up, he joined a secret service in the army. We never went in the pool, I never saw anyone go into the pool, it was disgusting.

Seven nights had passed, and Maria couldn't spend one night in the same room as Rose and me. On the last night she never came home at all. Up and down the old windy streets again in the bus to the airport, we all made it home safely.

Eddie and Rose took me up town to visit Edinburgh Castle. While looking over the ramparts, I found out I was scared of heights. The highlight of the trip was watching the one o'clock gun being fired.

Eddie had a heart attack. He was almost due to retire. He'd worked in the wire mill since he was 12. They gave him a set of cufflinks and a tie pin for his services rendered. Rose and Ed would go walking up Birstly Brae, along the fields at the bottom of Tranent and back to the house. It kept him off the drink for a while.

Rose Tranter made me a team leader at the playscheme. I was the only one who could stop the McLeod brothers from fighting. Andrew was a year older than me and David was a year younger, they were two big laddies. I got really friendly with them. They would come to my house and chat to Rose, she knew everyone.

Now that I knew the big secret, I was included in weddings and McGuire family parties. We had a fair-sized family in the Pans, it spread to Penicuik, Fife and Glasgow. There was a party in Glasgow one night where all the sisters dressed as fairies, Uncle Robert would sing, I enjoyed the banter. When the bus was leaving to go home, someone had to get Uncle Lackie. He was sick and flushed his false teeth down the toilet.

Chapter 15

I was up early for my first day at high school, this was a first for me. I even managed a bit of breakfast for the first time. It was a short walk to school; it was just around the corner really. As I walked in the gates there were older boys asking starters, "What does a boat do when it gets into harbor?"

The new pupils were saying, "What?"

"It pulls up!" They would grab their ties and throw them above their head. Nobody did it to me. We had to go to the assembly room, there were three houses – Gosford, Grange and Seton. Grange was for people who had family deriving from Prestonpans, Seton was for Port Seton and Gosford was Longniddry. I was put into Seton because no one in my family had ever been to Preston Lodge. Grange was full of panners because Prestonpans was the biggest catchment area. In registration, this guy called Brian Fee sat next to me. He went on to do it in every class. At break time, I met up with Ricky Adams for a wee walk around the school, we drew some size of entourage from the Prestonpans, Port Seton and Longniddry. I had come to secondary school with a huge reputation for being a hard cunt. They had heard stories about me from each of the main towns that attended the school.

Exactly two weeks into high school, I was almost at the doors leading to the boy's playground when this guy, Ian Brash, appeared from behind me.

"Am the bully o' the school."

"No bother."

"Everyone's gone about saying it's you, ya cunt, C'mon then!"

"You can be the bully, a don't want to fight again."

I turned around and walked out the doors that led to a wide flight of steps that went from one building across the playground to the other. There must have been about a dozen steps. Ian kicked me on the back, my bag, jotters and pencils went flying down the steps along with me. I managed to get up quickly and trap the advancing Ian in a headlock long enough for the woodwork teacher to eventually get there to break it up, I was choking the life out of him. I was told to report to the deputy headmaster's office first thing in the morning.

That was Mr Billsland, they called him 'Sasquatch' on account of the height and size of the man. I explained what happened as best as I could, but he was having none of it. He told me to stand up and put my hand out. I was barely two weeks into high school and this giant man was about to leather me with a strap made of leather. I thought, *here we go again*. He leathered me three times. I'd took his best shots, I could handle it, and I'd done nothing wrong. I was the first person in my year to get the belt.

What a start to my new school. I told Nana and Eddie the truth, I always told them truth. Eddie always told me, "It's an honest man's world, son." And I believed him 'til the moment that belt came crashing down on my hands three times. Nevertheless, I always believed what nana and Eddie told me.

At school they had been teaching us to play rugby. There were four teams made up of people who would potentially play for the first team, second, third and fourth. I was on the third and fourth pitch. I was running at Mark McGrath to tackle him when he put his hand out and thumped me in the face. I chased after him and started lashing at him 'til the teacher dragged me off. Both of us got sent over to the first and second pitch. Preston Lodge was a rugby-orientated school. You only got to play football for the school team in third year. I was made captain of the second team, we played on a Saturday at 9am in the morning. I played football in the afternoon, and then again on a Sunday. It kept me really fit and out of trouble.

I had a run-in at rugby training with a boy in my year called Stewart Torrance. He was twice the size of me, he wanted to fight me at the corner of the music department at dinnertime. I told him I wasn't interested in fighting anymore. At dinnertime, he followed me round the school and caught up with me at the music department corner, it was the way I was walking home from gym anyway.

"C'mon then!" he said with his pal standing next to him.

"Fuck off! I don't to fight."

He made a lunge for me. I quickly got him on the grass and started punching his face. His mate shouted, "Stop that!"

"I'll fucking punch you, ya cunt!"

He backed away. I got up and left Stewart lying on the ground with his face covered in blood.

I was to report to Mr Allan's office immediately, he was the headmaster, the last person I wanted to see. He told me Stewart Torrance had been to see him covered in blood.

"He jumped me from behind, sir."

"He has a witness, son."

"Aye! His best pal."

I spent as long as long as I possibly could trying to explain what really happened, Mr Allan was having none of it, no matter what I said. He had an array of belts he showed me. It was a foregone conclusion that I was getting the strap.

"Pick one of them, son."

I was now starting to panic because it was common knowledge Davey Allen could lay the belt. I had looked up to him so much, I never wanted to be in this position. I eventually, reluctantly picked one.

"Place your hand out, son."

I got three almighty whacks with the belt. I never cried; I was just disappointed that I got belted for something that wasn't my fault.

"You can go now, son. And I hope you've learned your lesson."

"Yes, sir."

I joined the tennis club with Billy Gray. He had a girlfriend who played tennis. We'd go to the furthest away court. I took it all seriously, everything I took part in I wanted to win. Billy was just looking for a muck-about, I was trying to serve like Bjorn Borg. I always had that winner's edge. Billy was just knocking the ball over; I was racing from side to side, diving to hit the ball where necessary on a tarmac court. By the end of our allotted time, the sweat was fleeing from me. Billy introduced me to his girlfriend's pal, Margo. We'd wait 'til everyone was gone and get a wee kiss in the bike sheds; it was my first kiss at high school.

At gym, I saw Roger Blake wearing a smart Hibernian strip. I liked the color and the sponsor's name so I asked Rose if she would buy me one. Surprisingly she bought me a real one, not a dodgy fake one from the Thursday market in Bonnyrigg. I just liked that particular strip to wear at gym time. Roger and I were having a laugh at gym, booting each other up the arse in a playful way. We were to form a line, he caught me a beauty, I rallied over to him and returned in kind. Bobby Davidson was our gym teacher; he must have only seen me placing the toe of my shoe against Roger's arse. Mr. Davidson kicked me really hard on the leg, he left me bruised.

"How do you like that, son?"

I said nothing, just got on with class. When I was home from school that day, I showed Rose. Apparently, John supposedly went down to school and made a complaint. There was nothing ever done about that incident. He probably never even got a warning. My reputation had proceeded me from primary school as one boy to look out for, but he was a fully-grown man knowingly kicking a boy. He obviously wanted a reaction, he never got one. I couldn't believe a teacher would get away with kicking a pupil who couldn't hit back. I hated Bobby Davidson after that...

Eddie had just finished painting his hut out the back garden green. I left it a few days then got hold of a small tin of paint and wrote 'ED' in big black bold letters on the door.

Rose paid for my school meals; she was too proud to go down the other route. I sold my 30p dinner ticket for 25p cash in hand so I could go up the chip shop at dinner time to get a chip butty and a game of space invaders. Mrs Findlay called me the bottomless pit; she must have thought I was also eating a school dinner.

I got picked for the school swimming team. Sid Gordon and I got the choice of front crawl or breaststroke. I could easily beat Sid at breaststroke, so I chose front crawl. It turned out to be a bad move. Sid got second in the breaststroke. I came last in the front crawl. It turned out the guy was Scottish champion. It was two laps of the pool, when I'd just turned around at halfway, he was getting out the water.

I never took part in school sports day apart from the obstacle race. Fully clothed I easily won. It was an embarrassment going up in front of everyone at assembly to receive a small black badge with a golden torch.

Jean Smile picked a handful of hopefuls every day during the summer to work at Lowe's fields. She was a good friend of Rose, so I kept getting picked every day. You could be doing anything from weeding to picking turnips. Jean gave me a pair of gloves.

The Hangout Youth Club was somewhere to go. We got to use the music classes and five-a-side pitch in the gym. We entered a team for a national competition. The preliminaries started in Bonnyrigg. Maria came along to see me play. I scored nine goals in one game and Isabel Mole substituted me. I was devastated, in a right mood. I gave her a piece of my own mind. Nine goals and getting substituted for a guy who had never played in a team in his puff. What was she thinking about? I was enjoying myself.

That was me finished with the Hangout for a while.

I liked going up to Musselburgh in the bus to see my old Uncle Jimmy, he was Eddie's brother. What a lovely man. I'd chat with him for a while then go down the main street where there was an alley that took you to a games arcade. I could never make it through to the end of this game called *Bomber* 'til I met a guy called Martin Telford. He showed me how to get to the end where you got another three lives to try again. He had mastered the game. He lived in Musselburgh. After a few more visits to see Uncle Jimmy, Martin helped me to conquer the machine.

A teacher slapped me in the face at school. Mr Ormiston was a big man compared to me; he was getting on in years but there was no need for his outrageous behavior. I only asked for a jabby thing.

"It's not a jabby thing, son, its's a chisel."

He caught me by surprise, I felt so embarrassed in front of the whole class, I was mortified, humiliated and broken.

The WAC under 13s had went Juvenile, this was Saturday football, not the Sunday churches league. I did play on a Sunday for the under 14s. We had a good pre-season and made a great start in the league. If you were going to get noticed by scouts of senior clubs, Juvenile League was the one to be in. I had been top goalscorer for the previous two seasons, and I was continuing in the same vein. On the way to training one night, I bought a Fifes Jubilee. It was a rectangular piece of frozen orange juice that was covered in plastic that was so hard you nearly pulled your teeth out trying to get it open. I was cutting it fine, training started in 10 minutes. I lay the Jubilee on the grass and took a bite after each exercise. One of the coaches, big Tam Paton, told me to throw the Jubilee away and concentrate on training. Nobody in their right mind would pay 10 pence for a Fifes Jubilee and throw it away.

"Naw!" I shouted

Tam said, "It's either the Jubilee or home."

"Well am away home, then."

I walked along the road, finishing off my crushed ice – the good part – and joined Meadowmill FC under 14s, back to the churches league. I played up front with Tattie Thomson.

I got kicked out of English. My reading and writing were that of a child. English always let me down, I couldn't read, I couldn't write. The teacher shocked me with his witty, smart remarks. When I was reading, all I could hear was the sound of laughter. In the last two years at high school, they didn't bother teaching me English, I was put into a class that was split in two and we had a quiz.

Chapter 16

Paul McGuire visited me.

"What's that pish you're listening to?"

"'Highway to Hell' by AC/DC."

"That's a load of shite, come to my house and listen tae some good tunes."

We went to Paul's, he put on an album called *Sound Affects* by The Jam, it was going change my life forever. I listened to every Jam album; they were amazing. The night after The Who played in the Playhouse, Edinburgh, I went up with Paul, Raymond Capaldi, Colin Ferrier, Robert 'Titch' Peden and Graeme 'Shep' Shepherd, to watch a film called *Quadrophenia*. It was about the mods and rockers in the 60s, it was the best film I'd seen. I knew that night I was defiantly a mod. Now I needed a pair of Sta Press trousers, a Fred Perry T-shirt and a pair of desert boots. Rose emptied every last penny out her purse. I was now officially a mod, one of the original eight from the top Pans. The only thing I needed was a fishtail parka, that was on the Christmas wish list – Santa Claus and all that shit.

I now hung about with the mods at school, they were in the year above me. It was the first time

I really felt a sense of belonging. It was the 80s mod revival, and I was part of it, I was living the dream. It was cool to be a mod, we were different from everyone else, something I knew about too well, but this was a good thing, the most positive characteristic move I had made 'til that point in my life. We would go through the corridors singing 'We are the mods! We are the mods! We are, we are, we are the mods'. Nobody could touch us; we were like the invincible. Raymond Capaldi had every color of Sta Press and Fred Perry T-shirts, boating jacket, desert boots, bowling shoes, parka – you name it, he had it. He was our proverbial leader. I went to his house with Paul McGuire. He not only had his own bedroom, he had a double bed, mirror wardrobes, big telly, video player and a cracking record player. His record collection was massive, it went from one side of the room to the other. He must have been the Ace Face in our wee mob.

All the mods were going to a party near Gullane, down the east coast, famous for its golf courses. It was an old house, looked like the green keepers, it was a wee bit tricky to find. I was told to be on the last bus home as per usual, everyone else was staying overnight. We did songs like 'My Generation'. I could see my girlfriend slipping into the arms of another guy. I lost the plot, walked over a few golf courses to the main town of Gullane, where I knew my mate, Andy Hume, would at an old school disco. It was pitch black,

I fell a few times, looked like I'd been working in the fields. My desert boots were ruined, that's what happens when you have a flash of madness.

I finally found the place, made my way past rockers in thick, black leather jackets and punks strewn about the floor inhaling glue bags. Andy was behind the decks, he was delighted to see me, there were lots of tidy lassies there. Andy was the main man, he got the DJ to play 'Green Onions', by Booker T & the MG's. I could dig this. There weren't any mods, so I did a solo on the dance floor, the girls loved it. I was dancing like Sting in the film *Quadrophenia*. I was really enjoying myself before Andy came up and said I'd better leave ASAP. The rockers, punks, rockabillies, the whole hall was filled with testosterone, I was public enemy number one. It was a brief appearance; it was emotional leaving my buddy. Andy and I made it to the car park. Just like Batman, Raymond Capaldi appeared on his 50cc scooter. I jumped on board; we were off like a shot. Back at the house party, this guy was now in the bedroom with my girlfriend. I was gutted, felt sad, but never fought over a girl. I got the last bus home, just like Rose had told me, I always did what Rose told me.

Chemistry class was so boring, the teacher went through the motions like a robot, he talked like a robot, maybe he was a robot. He kept leaving the class unattended. Mark McGrath was a rocker, Iron Maiden on the back of his denim jacket.

I was wearing Sta Press trousers and a white Fred Perry polo shirt. He was starting to piss me off with all his heavy metal shite, so I jumped on the table and did a rendition of 'My Generation' by The Who. The teacher walked in, I managed to get back down to my seat without too much attention. Mark and I were constantly winding each other up. The teacher called out, "Fraser! Can you explain this theory?"

"Fuck knows!"

"What did you say?"

"I've got an itchy nose..."

The class were in stitches, he wasn't impressed. "Get out of here! Go on, out my class!"

Mr Watson shoved me in the corridor, I shoved him back with great force. We literally fought for a brief moment before another teacher broke the fight up. That was the last time I saw inside the chemistry class, that was the last time I attended a chemistry class. I got booted out for misconduct, I didn't care, I was glad to see the back of that place.

The art class school trip to London was on Valentine's day. A lot of guys were sitting with their cards on the train tables right in front of them to show that they had at least one person who cared for them, I had never got a Valentine's card in my puff, we just played cards at our table. It was a long journey, at least seven hours.

London Underground was fascinating. You got a small map with different colored lines that all had different names so you could weave yourself to your destination. Our stop was Green Park near Piccadilly. I was sharing a room with Mark Smith and Belly. First thing we did was all the boys met up at McDonalds in Piccadilly Circus. Dukey said there was a bird looking at me called Karen Collins.

"Go up and talk to her."

"I don't know what to say."

"Just say hello, ya dafty."

I had always been shy with girls, Dukey was full of the patter, bold as brass, he didn't give a monkeys. Karen was in fourth year. On the way out we exchanged glances, I had the perfect opportunity to make a move, but I just smiled back and left the shop.

"Ya silly cunt, she was looking at ye!"

It was easy for Dukey to say, he'd been at it most of his days, I was an absolute beginner. I was one of the guys who had to get a pal to ask the lassie out and the answer was always no!

Most of the younger ones went to see Tottenham Hotspur play on the Saturday the rest went to the pub. We were right behind the goals of the Tottenham end of White Hart Lane and Scotsman, Stevie Archibald, scored the winner with a cracking header he almost burst the net; Archibald was class. The stadium was amazing compared to my beloved Tynecastle, home ground for Heart of Midlothian.

Chapter 17

The Duke asked Paul and I to come with him on the night he would become a fully-fledged member of the Orange Order. I didn't have a clue what he was on about, he made it such a big deal, he was counting down the days. It was to be held in Billy's Bar, just across the road from the chapel, that was next door to my old primary school, St Gabriel's. The Duke was following in his father's footsteps, his side of the family were Protestant and Lodge, the rest of us were brought up Catholic. Paul kept going on about having a black and tan to drink that night. Whenever Dukey brought the conversation up, Paul would start reminding us he was having a black and tan. I never had a clue what he was on about, the name just stuck in my head.

The three of us met at Duke's house on the night of the induction. The big day had arrived, Dukey's mum, Margaret, kept yelling at him, "Stop twirling the stick in the living room, son!"

Duke was in full throw, twirling his wooden flute band mace though his fingers, and back again, doing the same thing from hand to hand, around his back, he was great on the stick, I'd never seen him drop it once. He was just getting himself mentally prepared for whatever lay ahead that evening. In my house he would substitute his stick for one of my old golf clubs. Thankfully, there was nothing of real value he could break, just a collection of small wooden ornaments that were purely sentimental, he'd really go to town in front of Rose, she was his grandad's sister.

We walked to Billy's Bar from Dukey's house, an eerie silence fell as we got close, passing the chapel. Duke became all buoyant again as he heard the Protestant noise belting out. We walked through the gates of Billy's Bar, the place was massive, it looked like an old hotel, it was that big. We entered through a side door that took us to the King Billy's Bar, automatically you knew why it was named that as we turned and saw a large painting of King William of Orange adorning the wall as a centerpiece for all to witness. I made it clear to Duke that I didn't care what I drank, he gave me a lager tops. This was mainly a Scottish drink, it consisted of straight lager and a dash of lemonade. Paul got his black and tan, in all my life to come and pass, I never saw him drink so fast. We drank downstairs, then upstairs in a hall where everyone was gathered, then Paul and I were asked to wait outside. There was a hell of commotion coming through the walls, every kind of obscenity could be heard yelling and shouting. After a period of time, Duke stumbled into the corridor, Paul and I questioned him.

"Are you okay?"

"What the fucks that?"

"That's the Red Hand of Ulster"

Dukey had been slapped on the back by everyone in attendance, the mark left on his back was to signify something the Orange Lodge held so dear. It was an emblem on the flag of Ulster in Northern Ireland, a red hand. Dukey had finally managed to follow in his father's footsteps.

Chapter 18

I was a regular at the Annex disco in Musselburgh. My friend, Martin Telford, introduced me to a lovely girl called Tracy Allan. I walked her from the club to bus stop at the end of the night. She invited me to a party at her house.

On the night of Tracy Allan's party, I pulled on my skintight jeans, wore a pair of desert boots and a white Fred Perry underneath my parka. Tracy lived in Bank Park; I could see the private housing estate from the top of my street. Birstly Brae was a mile long, it was all uphill, it was the quickest way for me to get there. I had to walk over Prestonpans Train Station bridge, all the way up the hill to Tranent's posh area. I finally found her house, it was the first time I had walked in this location, the music was that loud I couldn't fail to miss it and the directions she gave me were bang on.

Her parents were away, it was full of Musselburgh mods, I was the only panner, and one of the youngest. The drinks were flowing, pictures being took, I sat on the end of the couch sipping a glass of water, I didn't drink. A lot of people were leaving the room. After a considerable amount of time there was just me and this girl who was sitting on a chair across from me. She had long blonde hair, was wearing a biker's jacket and jeans. I knew who she was, Mandy Vanbeck. She would walk past the Civic Square from time to time, all the mods fancied her. I had declared that I would go out with her one day. Nobody believed me, they knew I was talking shit. I was really shy but asked her where Tracy was.

"Upstairs."

"Thanks."

I left the room and went looking for Tracy. The party was definitely going on upstairs. I opened a few doors calling out her name. I opened this door and there were a host of people inside, on the floor and in the bed. I called out her name, she appeared from beneath the covers.

"I'll be with you in a minute."

"Okay."

On returning downstairs, Mandy was still sitting in the same seat. I went back to the end of the couch furthest away from her. My mind was racing, what was Tracy up to? I was meant to be her boyfriend...

"Come and sit over here."

"It's a single chair."

'Just sit on the arm."

Why was she asking me over, I was nothing special, I was younger than her, she could have anyone, and I was a mod. I went over and sat on the arm of the chair.

"I fancy you."

"But I'm meant to be going out with Tracy."

"She's not here is she? Give me a kiss."

Now I was really crapping myself...

"Am going to shite myself. What if Tracy comes in?"

"Do it quick, then."

The moment we touched lips I was in love, puppy love, but it was real to me. She led me by the hand upstairs and into this long, dark cupboard where there were lots of jackets hanging. Tracy was looking for me, she even shouted in the cupboard that Mandy and I were in. We were behind the jackets, kissing the face off each other.

The Moon Runners were a gang from Tranent, everyone hated them, even the Belters. They were trying to force themselves through the front door, gatecrash the party. Mandy told me to stay there. You could hear the Musselburgh mods getting their clothes on and running downstairs, they chased them up the road. Mandy and I slipped out the front door when no one was looking and went around the back garden. We held each other so tight while kissing behind the kitchen wall. It felt unbelievable, unreal, amazing, I was on cloud nine. After a period of time people started to fill the kitchen, I could see Tracy. Mandy asked if we were going out with each other now, I said yes! It was the easiest question I'd been asked in my life. I think I answered it before she finished the sentence. There was nothing to think about, I said it and I meant it, the deal was done in the back garden of Tracy Allan's house. Now we had to go back in the house and face the music. We must have been outside kissing longer than expected, the Musselburgh mods were leaving on scooters, and some making their way to the bus stop. Tracy was in the kitchen with her back against the fridge.

"Where did you go to?"

"Eh! Well..."

"Have you been with Mandy?"

I was too scared to answer.

"Well?"

No reply.

"Are we still going out?"

"Naw!"

"What do you mean, 'no'?"

"Ye were upstairs, and... Erm!"

Tracy started crying, I felt sorry for her. All that make-up running down her cheeks.

Mandy and I left the kitchen, outside we met her friend, Vince Kerr, who wore a black leather bikers' jacket and jeans. The Moon Runners were still in the vicinity so we had to be careful. I was wearing my fishtail parka but kept insisting I walked Mandy along the road halfway to her house. She was really against it, thought it would be too dangerous. She told me to wear Vince's jacket and she'd wear my park, surely, they wouldn't pick a fight with a girl. Vince was tall, his jacket drowned me. Mandy kept telling me not to worry, the thing is I would have done anything to spend a bit more time in her company. We held hands and she told me she was a librarian, I was still in fourth year at school.

We walked as slow as we could, getting to know each other. She was the only person who paid any attention to me at the party. Her long blonde hair almost touched the waistband on her jeans. I felt privileged to be walking hand in hand with such a stunning girl. I had my eye on her since the first time I saw her, all the mods reckoned I was going mad when I told them I'd go out with her one day. I couldn't stop looking at her, couldn't believe she would go for a mod who was younger than her and still at school. She talked about saving up for a motorbike, I didn't know how this would work with my dreams of owning my own scooter one day. I held on to her hand like it was the last time, I felt so alive, I honestly thought this was just a big dream, that I'd wake up any moment. It was real. Every Tranent mod was going to be so jealous of me. We kept stopping from time to time to reflect on how the night had gone, and also how Tracy must have felt. It was our night though and I was definitely milking the walk from Bank Park to the Chinese takeaway where I was to get the bus home. We passed the VG store, almost there. The feeling of saying goodbye was actually starting to hurt. We rounded the corner of the Keepers pub; we were almost there. I spotted Shep at the takeaway with a guy called Kev, who was deeply religious, he was really quiet. I thought I was safe now, so I gave Vince his bikers jacket back. Mandy wanted to stay with me, she was snuggling into my parka even though it was a warm night.

"You can go home now, Mandy."

"Are you sure? I'll wait if you want."

"Naw! It's okay now. Take care of her, Vince."

Mandy kissed me. I swear I could still feel those tender lips for about ten minutes after she'd gone. About ten minutes after she'd gone, the Moon Runners appeared at the Keepers Arms public house. There must have been about a dozen of them. Shep had a quick word with me.

"Don't look at them, Rainbow, they'll go away."

They walked down towards the Chinese takeaway. I remember Kev was leaning against the window, drinking a bottle of cola. One of them approached me.

"Are you Danny Galloway from Musselburgh?"

"Naw! Am Raymond Fraser from the Pans."

I heard one of them shout, "That'll do!"

A guy ran, jumped and kicked me in the face. I never went down. They had surrounded me, kicking and punching. I heard a bottle smash over my back. My parka had been pulled in so many directions it was completely over my head, I could see nothing. All I could feel were kicks and punches. Everything stopped when I heard this girl's voice. My parka was in disarray, I struggled with it to see where I was, it had shielded me from most of the blows. I was in the middle of the road. It was Wendy Raeburn, she took me to her sister's car, they drove to their home in Ormiston. I got offered a cup of tea. I didn't really drink tea, but I was grateful for anything after what just happened. I told Wendy and her sister everything that just happened. Even I was still confused why they'd picked on me; I was much younger than most of them. Wendy insisted I stayed at their house and slept on the couch.

"They're bullies."

I wanted to go back to the Pans, Wendy's sister offered to run me. I asked her to stop at Shep's house, it was just around the corner from mine. Shep answered the door. "Come in, Rainbow." It was just Shep and I, his big brother, Stuart, was still out. We discussed what went on in great detail. Shep told me that wasn't the end. "That bottle of cola they smashed over your back was Kev's, they put the broken bottle to his throat and said 'what are you going to do about it'."

Kev was a man of the cloth, he wouldn't hurt a fly, it just wasn't in him. Stuart came in, we went through the whole story again.

"There's nothing you can do, Rainbow."

Stewart was right. I left Shep's house, walked around the corner and had to go through the whole story with Rose again before I really appreciated putting my head on a nice soft pillow. I slept well that night. Mostly thinking about how I was going to meet up with Mandy. There was a lot of fighting up the bing between panners and belters.

My dad was in London, he had got married again. He was living in a place called Dagenham. I really missed my dad.

I was captain of Longniddry Villa, we beat Tranent in the final of the cup. I got to lift the trophy first in front of everyone. Jackie Raeburn was the manager, he said I was the best football player he'd ever signed.

Chapter 19

Everyone got in the minibus, we were heading for the Magnum Centre in Irvine, on the west coast of Scotland. It was 1981, it was the first time I was going to see The Jam. There must have been about a dozen of us, I sat next to Dolly Grey, he was one of the oldest on the bus, he was a mod, we were all mods. It was a long journey; it was worth it as we all huddled up right at the front of the stage pressed against the barrier. What a feeling of euphoria when they announced The Jam on the sound system. It was breathtaking watching them bounce high onto the stage holding their instruments, like something you'd more likely see at a gymnastics competition. Straight into their first number, the place was going mental. They were dressed in black suits, white shirts and black ties. This was The Jam, my favorite group, I could hardly catch my breath. Paul Weller was my favorite, Paul liked Bruce Foxton, the base guitarist, he said I looked like Rick Buckler, the drummer.

They began with a song called 'In the City', one of their older hits, then progressed through the years. Paul Weller was lead vocalist and lead guitar; I was only a few feet away as he belted out the classics. He was drinking a can of Red Stripe lager, he tossed the empty can into the crowd, a wild stramash ensued, they were like a pack of wolves fighting for it. Colin Ferrier emerged from the inner circle holding the can, he wouldn't show any of us, that could take pride of place on his bedside cabinet. After three encores it was all over, back to the minibus. On the way home, the bus broke down, everyone was panicking about making their work. Dolly didn't care, he'd booked the day off, I didn't care because I was still at school, I was the youngest on the bus.

The woven four-legged stool I made for my prelims in woodwork looked perfect the day before when I placed it on the rack. Someone obviously cut one of the legs off. The teacher, Chris Harvey, made a meal of it. He stood it on the workbench, it was clear as day there was half a leg missing, you could even see the rough saw marks. Anyone could see there was no way my stool was going to stand firm. I got kicked out of woodwork for that. Mr Harvey made a speech.

"I tell you this, Fraser. There's no way you'll make a penny from joinery. Don't expect to pay your way in life working with wood, you're useless. Forget about taking your exam, go now, don't come back. You'll never make a penny in this game; you'll NEVER work as a JOINER."

I heard Gerry O'Brian was ordained dux of the high school. Ever since I met Gerry, he could answer any question. And he could read a newspaper from a young age, when I thought a newspaper was for eating your tea on, so you didn't burn your legs. I could see that coming from a young age.

There were only two subjects I was interested at school, sports and art. I'd finished playing rugby and there was no more football so that journey had come to an end. I loved my art teacher, Mr Boyd, he was so funny and inspirational, art was the only prelim I passed.

Rose had somehow secured an apprenticeship with a building company from Musselburgh called G Grigg & Sons as an apprentice carpenter/joiner, I was to start work on Monday. A van would pick me up at the top of the road around 7:30am then take me to the yard. It was about a 20-minute journey sitting on benches that were either side in the back of the van. I was just a gofer, I'd go for anything the tradesmen asked for. I'd do the sweeping up and carrying all the rubbish bags down the stairs of tenement buildings in and around Edinburgh. Harry Grigg was paying me cash in hand – £15 a week. It only lasted a few weeks 'til Harry told me to come back when I get my P45 certificate.

Mr Boyd had sent a few people to my door asking me to sit my Art O level. I really couldn't be bothered with going back to school, all I wanted to do was start working. When school sports day arrived, I went down just to catch up with a few friends. The last event every year was the obstacle race, I had won that event every year since I was in primary school, but I was fully clothed. My mates encouraged me to take part anyway, so I took my place in the lineup, looking a little out of place with everyone else in shorts and a vest. The whistle blew and I was off like a shot, first to the net, first to everything. I never looked back 'til I broke the tape at the finish line. That was me finished with school right there, I didn't bother going back to pick up the winner's badge at assembly. I had made it through primary and secondary school undefeated at the obstacle race, I felt pleased with myself.

My P45 came through the door on my 16th birthday so I could officially go back to work at Grigg's, I got a cards from John and Maria and a wee present from Rose and Ed. Mr Boyd had been my biggest influence at school, I was gutted about letting him down by not sitting my art exam but all I could think about was starting work.

Prestonpans Legion under 16s had never lost a game all season, well, not when I played for them, I can be sure of that. We had to play Tranent at the Gyle in Edinburgh. If we won that game, we won the league. They played me up front that day, Joe Murray was shouting at the top of his voice, "Two of you mark him!"

As a corner came in, I moved around to find a better position and the ball was scrambled in Tranent's box. I toe-poked it into the net. Joe

Murray was going off his head, then Tranent got one back. We were all around the halfway line when the Tranent goalie kicked the ball up field, I could see the ball heading straight for me, Dukey screamed at me, "Go for it!"

I kicked the ball back towards the keeper and turned around, all my team mates were rushing towards me. The ball had gone over the goalie's head and right in the back of the net. Joe Murray looked like he was going to have a heart attack, shouting vile abuse at me. The referee had to have a word with him. Tranent managed to equalize but wee Rab Cochrane knocked in the winner.

After that game, the Pans Legion started playing me at right of midfield, I felt comfortable in this position and Johnny Cook said I was playing my best football. We had won the league with games in hand and were still involved in every cup. Well, that's what we all thought but it turned out someone had reported us for fielding an overage player. It turned out Michael Burns was around eight hours too old to play under 16 football. That was it, finished, we got stripped of the league title and booted out of every cup. I don't think anyone has really forgiven him to this day. One of my mates, who couldn't get in the team, asked me to come with him to train for Edina Hibs in the east side of Edinburgh. I had other ideas, I still had the notion of being a boxer, I always wanted to find out if I had what it takes.

Chapter 20

The alarm clock went off at 7am I got dressed and was at the top of my street by 7:30am. When we arrived in the yard, Harry told me to work with Ian Adams. He was refurbishing doors; the hut was cold and mostly loaded with junk. He stopped for exactly 10 minutes at 9am and half an hour on the dot at 12. I mostly hung about watching him work, it was tedious. The more I watched him, the more he began giving me jobs to do, using his tools. Ian was a grafter, a firm's man. Every time he went to the toilet, he said, "It's maybe not that big, but it's got a heed on it like a bothy cat."

I always thought there was a want about the guy. He was a good enough joiner but talked a lot of pish. His head was that far up Harry Grigg's arse you could almost see it popping out his throat.

"Let's see what Isobel's made me today."

Adams would go into every detail of what he had on his piece and you never had to buy a newspaper because he would give you a running commentary. Adams was a harmless man, a firm's man, I always got on well really with him.

Harry sent me to work with Bobby Grant, he was always laughing and joking, a big man with sweeping white hair and a white growth, he got the name Santa Claus. You needed a lot of tools working as a joiner, Harry gave me a canvass bag with some basic tools in it to get me started. The tools stayed brand new for a while except the axe and hammer, Bobby's favorite tool was the axe, he did most of his work with it. We were refurbishing an old tenement building in Newhaven in Edinburgh, it was right next to the water. Bobby glued an old heavy sink to the wall, propping it up with wood. He wanted to find out how strong the glue was. Next morning, he removed all the props, the old heavy sink was stuck solid to the wall. I was really impressed but wondered how he was going to get it down.

"The walls getting are plastered, son, get the sledgehammer."

Bobby was broad-shouldered, he was taking wild swings with the sledgehammer, it was down in no time, he'd also removed the thick layers of plaster right back to the bricks.

I met a second-year apprentice on the job called Paul Mooney, we always had a right laugh. His tradesman, Les, was around Bobby's age. Bobby was showing me how to lay floorboards, scribing them to fit against the wall with his trusty axe. There were some old floorboards that needed to be nailed down after the plumber had fitted new copper pipes upstairs in a house that was being lived in. Harry ordered me to do the job. I had watched how Bobby nailed either side of the flooring where the copper pipes were checked into the joist. After nailing the floorboard down, the laborers replaced the carpet. That was the first job I had carried out by myself, I felt kind of proud going home in the back of the van. Next morning, we found out I'd nailed a few pipes and flooded the flat below. I was standing with another apprentice joiner called Cheddar.

"In the name of the wee man!"

That was Cheddar's favorite saying.

When I saw Harry there was steam coming out his ears.

"Right, you! Down the road!"

I managed to get a loan of money for the bus back to the bottom Pans, walk up Coffin Lane to the bottom of Polwarth Terrace and the steep walk to my house at the top. It took a bit of explaining to Rose. I went back to work the next day, Harry was still in a mood, so I tried my best to keep out his sight.

Every Saturday I'd go with Prestonpans Hearts Supporters Club to watch my team, the famous Heart of Midlothian. Since I was working, I spent my money watching the famous. My dad had initially got me going to see them. Now it was my pal, Scott Grant, he was a diehard. With an average attendance of nearly six thousand, most punters headed to the terracing, making it a squeeze to get through the turnstiles. On days we got over

14,000. John Roberson was our top goal scorer in the league, we had been relegated to the first division, but wee Robbo was lighting the atmosphere like Chinese New Year, you could tell he was going to be something special.

The home corner of the terrace was covered by an old structural metal corrugated roof, we called it the shed. After making it through the turnstiles, Scott and I would make our way there. We always stood near Wattie the punk. He was unmistakable due to his colorful Mohican haircut and shaved head. He had a number one hit in Scotland with his band, The Exploited, called 'Fuck A Mod'. I was still more or less hanging onto my mod origins, still loved the music, but Wattie was cool, loud, and a proper Jam Tart, we called our team the Jam Tarts, because it rhymes with Hearts.

Scott and I would stand there shouting our tuppence worth of nonsensical abuse during the first half. At half time urine would run down the steps from the top corner toilet at the shed. After a few games, you just did what most people did, pish where you stood, queue up for a pie and listen to the man walking around holding a rectangular shallow box strapped around his neck, shouting, "Any Macaroons! Get your Macaroon bar here! Any Macaroons... Any Macaroons..."

Macaroon bars were very popular in Scotland, they were made here. It was made from white tablet covered in chocolate and coconut.

Hearts were trying to get back into the top flight of Scottish football with new manager, Alex McDonald, and John Robertson was battering in the goals to make sure we returned to our rightful place. Going to see the Hearts became a way of life for me, working hard through the week 'til Saturday came. Then it was on the supporter's bus singing my heart out. That's one thing I noticed about Hearts fans, win lose or draw, we all sang our hearts out on the terraces, shouting verbal abuse at the opposition where deemed necessary. I had money in my pocket, I bought new scarfs to wear with pride as my team got closer to promotion.

Matty Edmond got on the same supporter's bus, he was a few years older than Scott and me, he sat in the north side of the main stand. We would shout up to him as we made our way to the shed to stand in pish. Matty had his own seat, I could only dream of sitting in the main stand, the terraces were where the action was. You got a better view of the game from Matty's perspective, all the singing came from the shed. Nobody from Prestonpans Hearts Supporters Club got into fights at the football, it was just the game we loved, and all the banter that went with it. We were just proud to wear our scarfs; we were proud to be Gorgie Boys. The area that surrounded Tynecastle was called Gorgie, it was situated on the west side of Edinburgh. With John Robertson banging in the goals, Tynecastle – home to the famous Hearts – became a fortress. I followed my father; I spent my hard-earned money watching the famous Heart of Midlothian. Thanks to our strikers, John Robertson and Derek O'Conner, that season we secured promotion back to the top flight of Scottish football.

Chapter 21

Gerard McGuire and I met up at Prestonpans railway station. We travelled to Edinburgh Waverley where a connecting train took us to Glasgow Central. We were hanging around the main area of the station when Uncle Pat and Rab marched in wearing long black trench coats, they looked like the Mafia. We were bundled into a waiting car and took to the Railway Club in Barlanark. The place was bouncing, it looked rough, like stepping back in time to the Wild West. We were not in long before a fight broke out on the other side of the dance floor. This guy was chasing an off-duty police officer around the hall, brandishing a chair above his head. He launched the chair at the fleeing policeman, it whacked Gerard on the back of the head. Gerard looked slightly precarious as we left the club.

Once we got home, he was nursing his wound with a frozen bag of peas, still looking a tad concussed. Uncle Pat was a genius at turning any given scenario into a right good laugh. Gerard and I ended up sharing a double bed. In the morning, Uncle Pat and Cousin Pat were lounging in the living room wearing matching fluffy white bath robes. I thought they looked smart; it was much better than sitting in a pair of pants. Auntie Betty came through with cups of tea, young Pat's mug had a personalized name on it. Uncle Pat burst into life again.

"Are you still playing football, Raymond?"

No! I'm going to try boxing; I want to find out if I have what it takes."

"That's good, son, the laddie, Mallon, round the corner's boxing."

"I need to find out, Uncle Pat."

"Go for it, son. You'll never know 'til you try it."

Between making cups of tea, washing our clothes and making breakfast, Auntie Betty was constantly in and out the kitchen. Our wee cousin, Roseanne, was playing music from a tape recorder. There was one particular song I could have listened to all day called 'Promised You A Miracle' by a band from Glasgow called Simple Minds. I kept asking Roseanne to play it, I'd not been paying much attention to the charts since I started grafting.

That evening we were going to the labour club with our cousin, Pat, we were meeting Big Bob in there. A sprightly walk, running parallel with the motorway, we were there in no time. I always looked young for my age, so I thought there was no chance of getting in, Pat kept reassuring me. "You'll be fine, Raymond, don't worry, cuz."

It was easy for Pat to say, I was shitting myself. We made it in okay – that was huge weight off my shoulders. Big Bob got a round of drinks in. Apart from going to the bar, we sat at the same table all night drinking pints of lager, we must have drunk about 15 pints. Walking out the club was easy 'til the fresh air hit me, I could not feel my legs, my head felt dizzy. Pat gathered us together. "It's okay, cuz, you're just drunk."

The last time I felt like this was when I won a bottle of González Byass wine from the summer fair and drank it at New Year. Gerard looked in some state too. While staggering up the road, Pat noticed police walking in our direction on the lookout for underage drinkers. He got in the middle of Gerard and I, trying to steer us discreetly on the path in a straight line, I never thought we'd make it home, but Pat could handle his drink. We finally made it back to Uncle Pat's tenement, negotiated the stairs and we were home. Pat shot off to meet up with a girl. My head hit the pillow; I was out for the count.

All of a sudden, I felt like I was going to be sick. I rushed to the toilet. Gerard was sitting on the pan with his pants round his ankles with diarrhea, while spewing profusely into the sink, it wasn't a pretty sight. Immediately I ran to the kitchen, the basin was piled high with plates, for a split second I thought the walls were going to get a bodily makeover. I could feel the sickness erupting in my stomach while frantically lifting dishes from the sink. I just managed to clear the last plate when an explosion of vomit left my mouth at the speed of light. Thought I was never going to stop, while running a tap, swishing spew down the plug hole.

Auntie Betty walked in. "Are you okay, son?" It was extremely hard to apologize while I was still vomiting into her sink. The pain was excruciating, Betty was rubbing my back. "C'mon, son, get it all up." I felt like I'd lost half my bodyweight, my stomach cramps were almost unbearable. "Just you go back to bed, son, I'll clear this up."

I woke up in the morning with my head banging. I suddenly felt this cold slimy feeling sticking to my back, the room was stinking. Gerard had spewed on my back in the middle of the night. He'd got up first and blamed it on me for being sick in the bed. How on earth could I be sick on my own back? It was a busy bathroom that day. The two Pats were sitting in their fluffy white bath robes, Betty had to wash all our clothes that day.

"Do you still want to be a boxer, Raymond?"

"Awe, aye, Uncle Pat, that's me finished with the drink."

He nearly fell off his seat laughing.

Uncle Pat got us a lift back into Glasgow Central train station. All the way home to Prestonpans, Gerard was still denying he was sick on my back.

Chapter 22

I stood at the bus stop waiting to go to Meadowbank. The nerves were kicking in. I had punched the stuffing out an old army bag at the weightlifting club but now I was going to a real boxing gym. I was paying my own way; I'd worked hard for the chance to see if I had what it takes. I was using my own money; I was finally in a financial position to make my own decisions. It was a month off my 17th birthday; I was a late starter in boxing terms. I knew very little about the teachings of boxing apart from that small stint when I was eight years old, and what I had watched on the telly over the years since my childhood. The bus drew up and I paid my fare, there was no going back now. It travelled through Wallyford, Musselburgh, Joppa, and into Edinburgh, passing Jock's Lodge to Meadowbank. I asked how much it was to go to boxing and the lady told me £1.50, so I asked her how much for track and field, she replied 50p – that was a third of the cost.

"One for track and field, please."

I'd saved myself a pound, I knew where I was going from when I came running with Scott

Grant, I was determined to walk through the doors this time.

The gym was busy, it looked like the seniors were sparring and the rest were punching a bag or skipping. This small man wearing glasses came up to me and introduced himself as Benny, he asked if I was a new starter.

"Aye."

He took me to the equipment cupboard and found a pair of skipping ropes. I skipped for ages; it was murder. I could hardly skip three on the trot. Then I put on a pair of boxing gloves and found a bag. I was never shown what to do or how to punch, everyone looked like they knew what they were doing. Old Benny asked me if I wanted to spar.

"Aye."

Still a youth, I got asked to enter the ring. I was just lunging at my opponents with no clue of what I was doing. The boys nicknamed me Rocky cause of my wild punching style.

A couple of weeks passed; I didn't seem to be getting any better. I wondered if I was in the right game. Nobody had showed me a thing about boxing, I did lose a few pounds in weight punching the bags, circuit training and skipping. I was confused, boxing was not what I'd remember it to be. I was coming home on the bus feeling like I was drunk, sitting at the back laughing to myself for no reason.

Tombo wanted to come along to boxing. We had a right laugh on the way home after knocking lumps out of each other. He said the feeling was better than drink. I asked old Benny why I was feeling drunk on the way home. He told me a cloud in your brain had to develop so you could withstand the punches. Trying to walk in a straight line coming off a bus while it was moving was a laugh. You never received constant blows to the head playing football, this was something completely different from kicking a ball, I wanted to find out if I had what it takes, so I kept going to Meadowbank three times a week to find out.

My tick-tock alarm clock would ring in the morning. I would get ready, grab the sandwiches Rose had made me from the fridge and head up to the top of the road where I met Jimmy the dog. He was always there first. The Grigg van would pick us up and take us to the yard. Bobby Grant would tell me what materials to get then we'd be off again to the building site. I'd still be sweeping up and lifting bags of rubbish down three flights of stairs. I helped scaffolders and roofers and occasionally, getting time to watch Bobby work. I had a full bag of tools but mostly used my cold chisels and an axe. The axe was Bobby's favorite tool, he used it for cutting flooring, scribing door facings, almost anything you could ordinarily just use a saw for. It was much better working with Bobby and Jose, you always got a good laugh. I always came home looking like I'd been down the pit. That was the last place Rose had wanted me to go, all her brothers were miners.

My 17th birthday came. I just got a card John, and Maria said I was over 16 and too old for presents, so I got a card from her. Rose and Ed always gave me a present. My dad was in Dagenham, London, 500 miles away. I wondered how he was getting on; I hadn't seen him in two years.

Auld Benny told me he had tried to enter me for the Scottish Youth Championships but I'd only been boxing for a few weeks. Now that I had turned 17, he had me matched up for a fight at Gorebridge Miners Welfare Club against a guy from Bonnyrigg called Billy Martin at senior level. These revelations came as a surprise to me, I had not long started at the club, now I was to step through the ropes on a show in front of a crowd of people. I thought about it every day and night, I even dreamed about it, couldn't get it off my mind no matter what I was doing at work or in the gym. All I thought about was having to step through the ropes. And you always had to keep an eye on Brad Welsh when you were on a bag, he was the smallest boxer in the club, weighing about eight stone. He'd go around digging guys in the kidneys until he managed to get on a punch bag. It was funny to watch, though, he never bothered me at 11 stone, but you had to keep an eye out for him anyway.

The pressure was building every day, I was counting the days and hours 'til I had to step in the ring. Maria was coming to the show, she said she'd give me a tenner if I won my fight.

I went to bed earlier than usual the night before the fight, almost choking on second hand pipe smoke that engulfed the bedroom from John being on his ham radio sending Morse code signals all over the world. Cigarette smoke in the living room to pipe smoke in the bedroom, what chance did I have? I must have eventually dosed off after overthinking about what lay ahead.

My alarm went off in the morning, the room still stunk of smoke, I felt sluggish and tired from grafting a six-day week, I always had a long lie-in on a Sunday. Boxing Day had arrived, I was so nervous, the butterflies in my stomach were going ten to the dozen almost overwhelming me with frightening emotion. I had to wake myself up by splashing my face over and over, patting cold water on the back of my neck, this was nothing like playing football – you were the whole team. I wasn't sure if I was prepared, maybe my opponent wouldn't turn up? There were lots of formulations going through my head. I got my clothes on and packed my bag, never had a breakfast in case I had to weigh in, and made my way by bus to Meadowbank – that's where the minibus was picking the team up. Before you knew it, I was in Gorebridge in Midlothian, on the outskirts of the city. I was fighting in the first half of the show. We got there early so I had plenty time to dement myself even further. The spectators were arriving, the hall was beginning to fill up. Maria was sitting near the bar having a few drinks on the opposite side to the changing rooms. I went up to speak to her, she said she was really nervous, she was drinking vodka. Auld Benny came up to me and said I had to make my way to the changing rooms, he reassured Maria, "Don't worry, he'll be all right."

My cornerman, Graeme White, was waiting for me in the changing rooms, he told me to get ready quick because a few fights were off the card. I got ready sharpish, pulling on the maroon-colored vest of Meadowbank. I needed the toilet so much that I just kept sitting in the toilet.

"Raymond Fraser! Gloves on!"

It's now or never, I kept saying to myself. This guy put a pair of boxing gloves on me and indicated to the ring, saying, "You're on next." I was back in the toilet, now I was struggling to pull down my shorts and pants wearing gloves, frantically trying to get the thumb part of the glove under the shorts, eventually just sitting there, nothing was coming out. I felt so alone, the place was buzzing with noise.

"Raymond Fraser! You're on now..."

I had to get Graeme to give me a hand pulling up my shorts. We made our way through the crowd to the boxing ring; I could hear Maria screaming, "Kill him, Raymond!"

We approached the ring; it was only a few steps 'til I made my way through the ropes. I felt a kind of relief once I was bouncing on the canvas starring across the circled square at my opponent, thinking, *you're getting done, pal.* That's all I could think about as the referee called us to the center to give his instructions. We touched gloves and went back to our respective corners. Graeme was giving me instructions while placing my gum shield in, all I could think about was, *he's getting done.* I felt really aggressive, like a raging bull.

The bell rang, we both rushed towards each other, standing in the middle of the ring for three minutes, trading blow after blow. We could have fought in a telephone box. You couldn't hear the crowd, it was just like a square go except you could only use your fists. The referee had to pull us apart, apparently the bell had gone. I walked back to my corner and sat on the stool that Graeme had provided. He told me to dance around, I was like the Honey Monster when I tried that kind of thing. Graeme kept shouting instructions, they were going in one ear and out the other. The bell rang again, I did the same as in the first round, met my opponent in the middle of the ring, trading blow for blow. This was just a punch up, the referee stepped in and said something about going back to the corner.

"What's happening, Graeme?"

"The fight's been stopped, son."

"Who won?"

"You won, Raymond."

To be honest, I never had a clue what was going on most of the time, it was all just a blur in my mind. It never really made sense or sank in 'til

I was called back to the middle of the ring. I could feel the strong grip of the referee holding my wrist, then the voice of the ring announcer.

"The winner, by second round stoppage, in the blue corner from Meadowbank, Raymond Fraser!"

The referee lifted my arm high in the air. What a feeling! It was like a lightning bolt of euphoria shot through my body, I'd never felt like this in my life. I could now acknowledge the crowd and I could also hear Maria screaming. My opponent, Billy Martin, didn't look happy, it was his home show. We touched gloves, but I could tell he was gutted. We definitely put on a show of some sort although I don't think it was a pretty sight seeing as I never knew what I was doing myself, I was just fighting on instinct. The trophy I got was around a foot tall, it was really smart, I couldn't wait to put that on top of the drawers that I had built in my own room.

Maria had a good drink in her when we finally met up after I got changed, she said she was constantly back and forth to the bar and thought she was going to miss my fight due to the number of times she went to the toilet. A ten-pound note was handed over, as agreed. I didn't want to take her money but she insisted, she told me she'd give me ten pounds every time I won a fight; It wasn't an incentive but a tenner was a tenner, eh.

Eric White told me to watch a fight that was happening. He said that the guy called Graeme

Diggins in red colours from Haddington ABC was being lined up as my next opponent. I never paid much attention; I was far too busy enjoying winning my first fight. Maria told me she almost got thrown out for shouting, I could easily understand that.

Rose was well chuffed when I came home and told her the news. She was never one to give me praise for anything, she always put me down no matter what I achieved; this time I could tell she was proud of me. She took the trophy and placed it right in the center of the shelf above the fireplace. Eddie actually spoke, he rarely spoke without a drink.

"Well done, son."

Chapter 23

I'd been jogging since I turned 16 so I entered myself for the Prestonpans half-marathon. There were runners from all over the Lothians and Edinburgh who competed in all half-marathons throughout the summer, it had become like another stage of the circuit to them. I'd been running for around 20 minutes a few times a week and this race was over 13 miles. Castlepark Bowling Club held the event. Surprisingly enough, I got there really early, I was always late, Rose would say I'd be late for my own funeral. I had plenty time to get changed and made sure I went to the toilet. I jostled for a decent starting position to give myself a wee chance before the race began in earnest.

It was the first time I'd ever paced myself in a long-distance run while keeping close sight on the leaders. I began sweating profusely with the sun beating down so strong that sweat was nipping my eyes, pushing myself harder and hared 'til I made it to the finish line. Sitting exhausted on the grass, this man came up to me and said I was third. I was a wee bit bewildered 'cause all I was trying to do was keep an eye on where I was going and watching my knees lift, I wasn't paying attention to my whereabouts regarding position in the race. At the awards ceremony, I got a bronze medal. It was engraved, I was delighted. I had always sprinted into the lead at school during long distance running then drastically burnt out in the latter stages. I walked home proudly with the medal hanging around my neck. Rose and Ed never made a big fuss but I'm sure deep down inside they were proud of me.

One hell of a head cold floored me before a rematch with Billy Martin at his home show in Bonnyrigg. Benny decided to let Tombo step in for his first fight. He'd started boxing before me, we sparred together, it made sense.

On the day of the fight, I felt a bit better. They wouldn't let me go in Tombo's corner because I could still pass on the remains of my symptoms, so I had to be a spectator.

Tombo looked confident as he made his way to the ring in his brand new predominantly green shorts that had a white stripe either side.

The first round was a brawl. Right as the bell went for the second, Billy almost ran across and clocked Tombo a beauty that sent him flying back into his own corner. The fight was over, Tombo looked dazzled and distressed. In a state of disarray after the official verdict, he shunted out the ring with fierce anger and rage.

I went to his house after the fight, couldn't console him. He was in a right state about his trophy. It had 'runner up' engraved on the plinth. An idea eventually struck me, so I picked up the trophy that sat proudly in the middle of the living room window and ripped off the metal tag.

"It's a winner one now, who's going to know?"

"Me."

"Aye! But nobody else will."

My sudden flash of genius seemed to do the trick. He was all smiles again.

A few weeks later I got sunstroke, it put the rematch with Martin in jeopardy once again. I was itching from head to toe, always got prickly heat through the summer, but this was unbearable, doing squats against the wall to appease my back while using both hands on my body and legs. The pain I was going through was unbelievable.

My back was still peeling when I turned up at Wester Hailes in Edinburgh for the rematch, covered in aftersun. Almost shit myself when it sunk in that the ring was in an open air school car park with the sun beating down. All I was worried about was finding suntan lotion. Then I found out Billy Martin hadn't turned up.

I was top of the bill, doing an exhibition with the Scottish youth champion, Lee Maxwell. I was slightly older; Lee had more experience and was slightly heavier. The bout was on and off so much, Lee was a bit anxious. My back was peeling, Graeme White was slapping on suntan lotion, the highest factor we could find. It was still itchy as we walked through the crowded car park towards the ring. All Lee's family and friends had come to see him. It was an extraordinary hot day; you could have fried an egg on the ground. Lee finally made it to the ring, thank the Lord. I was boiling in almost freakish Caribbean weather.

After two relatively hard rounds, Graeme told me Lee didn't want to come out for the third round, so I quickly said, "Water!"

I beckoned Lee out of his corner using my hands, he looked tentative, slowly moving towards me. Just before we engaged, I spat the mouthful of water into his face. It seemed to lighten things up. Both of us delved into a right carry-on inside and outside the ropes. Instead of punches we were throwing water, the boxing ring was like a swimming pool. The judges wanted to give us 'Best Fight of The Day' trophies, even though it was only an exhibition. What was meant to be only a light-handed affair became a grueling contest, then a pantomime.

Lee went on to win multiple Scottish titles at heavyweight and super-heavyweight. The pinnacle of his career took him all the way to London's Albert Hall in the finals of the British Amateur Championships.

Chapter 24

We all got moved to a building site at Juniper Green in Edinburgh. It was a big job for G Grigg & Sons, it was a priority job for Harry. Including myself, there were three apprentice joiners, the other two being Jimmy Scott and Gary Hood. We were all quite shy and quiet to begin with, it was a new experience for us, straight out of school, none of us had a clue what was going on. Jimmy got the job of going to the shops at dinner time for every worker on the site, it was pandemonium. He never managed to get the orders right; the boys were giving him it tight. He got called every name under the sun, eventually they just called him Jimmy the Dog, he didn't last long in that job.

Gary was up next. He lasted a bit longer than Jimmy. Similar to Jimmy, he was getting the change wrong. He had this thing about Mars bars. When anyone asked him to get them something with the change, he always bought Mars bars, there was a lot of moaning and groaning about that. It all came to a head when he was given a £10 note for a meagre number of snacks, for the worker's treat he bought him 20 cigarettes – the guy never smoked. Maybe he should have got him a Mars bar. He had pushed them beyond reconciliation; I was next to walk the line. What a difference, everyone was getting what they ordered, and the exact change into the bargain. Bobby Grant had showed how he would go about going to the shops. I got a loud cheer from all the boys on the site that day. I had a lot to thank Bobby for, his system had paid dividends so much I got the job every day.

Jimmy was first to be initiated by the boys. The main protagonists were Stewart 'Purdy' Purves, Derry 'Del Boy' Livingstone and Cheddar. I could never remember Cheddar's real name, everyone called him that, he was just Cheddar. I watched Jimmy being dragged up the stairs to a house Purdie and Del Boy were working on. There was a lot of commotion, all you could hear was Jimmy shouting, "HELP! HELP!"

All the boys on the building site downed tools to witness this hilarious scenario unfold. Jimmy came running down the stairs naked, covered in white glue and sawdust. He was running everywhere, like a headless chicken, 'til he eventually climbed into a steel barrel full of dirty water the plasterers used for cleaning their tools, bobbing around scratching like mad. I felt bad for Jimmy, it must have been so embarrassing, he was struggling to clean himself. Apparently, this was all part of the initiation process.

Harry's two brothers, John and George, worked on their own projects. John had taken a liking to

Gary, he was off the site like two shakes of a lamb's tail.

Rose bought me a brand-new boiler suit so I could keep my clothes tidy. I maybe never had a clue what was going on at work, but I looked the part.

While taking snack orders for the shop from the boys, I felt a bit tentative around Purdy, Del Boy and Cheddar. They were always up to something, you had to have eyes in the back of your head. I got lured into the same upstairs house where Jimmy fell victim. Doogie, the plasterer, happened to be there with lorry driver, Jock Sutherland. Unwittingly I thought this would save me some time looking for them. All of a sudden, like a pack of wolves, they ruined me from every angle. In the blink of an eye, I was lying flat, like Jesus being nailed to the cross, except these were six-inch nails driven through my boiler suit, arms and legs, then left to the mercy of Purdy, Del Boy and Cheddar. Purdy leaned over, slashed my boiler suit open with a Stanley knife, then began to take my clothes off. I felt helpless as he undid my trouser belt, stripped me to the knees. Cheddar was gathering sawdust; Del Boy had a large tub of wood glue in his hands making his way towards me. Just for that brief second, I thought, *I am a goner*. Then I summoned all my strength, ripped through the nails, pushing Purdy over while gathering up what clothes I had left. I pulled up my pants and trousers while making a sharp exit to the door and made my way to freedom.

Make no bones about it, the initiation ceremony was a terrifying ordeal that I wouldn't wish upon anyone. My brand new boiler suit was ruined. On the other hand, Purdy, Del Boy, Cheddar and everyone else had accepted me as one of the boys.

There was a more relaxed feeling on the site. Everyone seemed to be more approachable. The upstairs house was a pleasant place to go, Purdy took time to show me his smart wooden toolbox, which was his pride and joy. He had various sorts of tools for chiseling and drilling holes. I really wanted one, he said he got it from a catalogue. I harped on at Rose to buy me one just like it from her catalogue, it was out of my price range, so I suggested maybe a birthday present or Christmas. I was getting paid £27 a week, £15 in dig money never left me much. The toolbox looked really smart and expensive. No matter what I suggested, she was having none of it.

Purdy asked for sky hooks, never had a clue what they were. Asking almost everyone I could see, they just directed me to some other tradesman, felt like I was going around in circles until I reached Bobby Grant. Bobby always told me the truth, he could hardly contain himself, I could see the signs etched all over his face as he blurted out who to ask. I was extremely naive; this was all new to me. I told the apprentice plasterer, John, who lived just up the road from me in

Tranent. He went on to say, "There's no such thing as sky hooks, you can't hook nothing on to the sky. When I started, they sent me for a bucket of steam."

It all began to make sense now; Purdy had got me, hook, line and sinker. Purdy and Del Boy were pissing themselves laughing. Purdy picked up a hand tool lying on the floor and declared that this was the fifteen-minute rule. If anyone leaves a tool lying near him unattended for fifteen minutes, he put it in his toolbox, because he proclaimed himself to be 'The Collector of Tools'.

The days and weeks were passing, everything was going great until I came back from the shops one day. I got every order correct except Harry's.

"I asked for a sausage and egg roll, there's no egg!"

You could hear a pin drop in the canteen. This was the first time I got an order wrong, and Harry was the boss. He made a right song and dance about it.

"Son, you can just take yourself down the road; beat it!"

I respected Harry, even liked him as a person, but didn't like the way he went about things. I never had enough money to get home, had to kindly ask the boys to help me with bus fares.

It took three bus journeys to get home from Juniper Green. It took that long to get home there was not much difference in time from any other day. Rose asked me, "Where's your boiler suit?"

"Eh! It's in the plastic bag."

"What's it doing in there, son?"

I had to tell Rose the truth, I always told her the truth. She was fuming.

"I just bought you that."

"I know."

"Well, that's your last, son."

Getting sent home hurt, but I still went to work the next day, and got sent to work with Jock Purves, Purdy's father, who was a painter and decorator. Jock was a great laugh, full of nonsense. I was enjoying myself again, happy days!

Eventually I got moved to the workshop, making doors with Ian Adams. I could have done without the constant smell of glue and breathing in the fine particle of cut wood that would circle the air.

At break time outside the workshop, it was so hot that day I sat on a mound of sand. A laborer called John kicked off about boxing and this guy who taught boxing at the Wallyford Institute called Bob Scally. He told me Bob was Scottish professional champion and chief sparring partner to Tommy Farr from Wales, who went 15 rounds with the great Joe Louis. Louis was world champion for 12 years, a lot of boxing scribes thought Farr had edged it on points that night. While sparring in the Catskill Mountains, New York, the press proclaimed it should have been Scally who went in with the legendary Louis that night. I was on the verge of packing in boxing, intrigued with John's story so much, I decided to give it one last go.

Walking into the institute, I noticed a lot of guys seeking the wisdom, they were all heavier than me.

"Can I help you, son?"

This voice seemed to come from nowhere.

"Can I help you son?"

I looked everyone straight in the face, up, down and all around then I noticed a big man hanging from a rope dangling from the ceiling. He was built like a bull. His descent was equally as impressive as seeing him aloft. This broad-shouldered proud-looking man with a neck that thick you couldn't hang him. He walked over to me.

"Are you Bob Scally?"

"Aye, son!"

"Will you train me to fight?"

Bob looked me up and down. "I'll teach you, son. Monday, Wednesday, Friday at the institute, Tuesdays and Thursdays at Sparta in Edinburgh."

"Aye! All right."

Bob started with my feet then worked his way up. He seemed to hone in on me after he found out who my dad was. Alec Kelly was his partner; he was also a Scottish professional heavyweight champion. They were both big gentlemen. There were no punch bags, nothing, just a big empty hall. Bob encouraged me to dance around a segment of the hall that was taped like a badminton court – that was our ring. We worked on footwork, dancing around the square, shadow boxing. He was a perfectionist, studying every move I made and correcting me accordingly. I would blunder my way around the ring at Meadowbank without a clue. The method Bob used got the juices flowing, I was floating like a butterfly. Every time I met Bob and Alec, I wanted to better myself.

Instead of getting the bus up to Wallyford, I would run with a rucksack on my back holding my skipping ropes, a towel and a change of clothes. I'd partner another person to work on punching techniques, Bob was never far away, instructing me every minute of every round. We practiced blocking, parrying, slipping punches and counterpunching. Almost from the minute I waked through the doors of the institute, I felt like I was getting somewhere. Bob instilled great belief, a professional mindset and the greatest amount of confidence I'd ever known in my life, I felt invincible. Bob was old school, offensive, defensive, he had a remedy, he had every trick in the book. I was that dedicated by the motivation, encouraged and self-belief he instilled in me that I started to run to and from training.

My fitness levels were going through the roof, every Sunday I'd go on an unusually long run. I mentioned to Chalky White about steel toe caps for running, he would sign an extra pair out and give them to me. I did all my running using them to weigh my legs down, Chalky was always on hand with another pair at the ready. My dad ran using steel toe caps when he was in training for a fight so that's what I did. My weight slipped from 10 stone, 7 pounds to 10 stone in no time. I began sparring guys who were 11 stone and ended up sparring the club heavyweight. I gave him lockjaw with a left hook. He wouldn't spar with me again, so big Alec had to step in, he became my sparring partner. All the boys at the institute would gather to watch, I started to get a bit cocky, winding my right arm up by throwing it in circles then landing a straight left, big Alec didn't look amused, the boys were in tears of laughter. I committed to a straight left, overhand right, followed up by a left hook. The combination was bang on, Alec sort of stalled for a moment then beckoned to come close to work on his body. He got me in a headlock, rattled me on the jaw with a short clubbing right hook then threw me away.

"That combination you hit me with would have dropped anyone your weight, Raymond."

I couldn't open my mouth, I just had to nod, I had lockjaw. I went to the toilet and couldn't get my gum shield out my mouth. Alec was a fair man, a god-fearing man, a truly divinely righteous man, someone to look up to. I took my medicine well, couldn't eat for a couple of days. I learned my lesson the hard way, there was no other way for me.

During lockjaw, there was a scaffolding pin left in the wall at work, it wasn't far from the roof of a tenement building on London Road, Edinburgh, it was left there by mistake. They weren't going to build a new scaffold to get it out, so Jock suggested Digger held my legs while I chiseled it out.

"No way! I'm scared of heights."

"You'll be fine."

"I'll no' let you go, Raymond."

Famous last words, eh. I was game as a trout about anything but not heights. Jock and Digger were urging me, daring me. Digger kept reiterating, "I swear, I'll no' let you go. If you don't look down, you'll be fine."

Digger looked like a strong man; I was sure of that.

"Let's do it, then."

Jock started tying a rope around Digger, I could have done with one myself.

"What about my rope, Jock?"

"You'll be fine, Raymond, I need to harness Digger, he'll be holding your weight. We don't want the two of you going over the top."

I was lucky I'd lost a few extra pounds with the lockjaw by not eating my sandwiches at work and my tea was down to a Cup A Soup. Jock tightened the rope; Digger held my legs. As Digger lowered me, I just kept staring at the gable end of the building. Hammer and chisel were in action, Digger shouted, "HURRY UP, IM GONNA DROP YOU!"

I had the pin out in a flash. Digger lifted me back onto the flat felt of the roof then started rolling about laughing with Jock. I thought they were happy we'd pulled it off. Digger could hardly get his words out. "I was only joking, Raymond; I was never going to drop you!"

I told Paul Mooney, he said he'd never do it because Digger had been in jail for murder. It was a sobering thought, the job was done, I trusted Digger with all my life. Paul Mooney and I had decided to go to Blackpool for the September weekend.

Chapter 25

Pau Mooney was waiting for me as I got off the bus at Pinkie in Musselburgh. I slept under a cross that night, and a picture of the pope. In the morning, Paul's dad dropped us off behind St James' Centre at the main bus terminal where we embarked on our adventure to Blackpool. We sat there like two schoolboys on their way to the Playboy Mansion. Blackpool was as close as it got to seeing a bit of action. The digs were not bad considering the price we paid. It was long and narrow with a double bed that consumed the width of the room. I always slept next to the door, Paul was going to have to get in first or climb over me. Nearest the door was an old cabinet with a mirror, a chair, and a decent sized bathroom.

That night, before going out, Paul was at the mirror with a pair of scissors, chipping a bit of his fringe, he called it the 'coo's lick' look, so I had a go too. We were like brothers from another mother. Our bed and breakfast was closer to the Pleasure Beach, so we paid to get into a disco above it that was near deserted. Haircut 100 were a one-hit wonder pop group who had a catchy hit 'Love Plus One', they kept playing it over and over, we ended up strutting our stuff together after a few drinks. Marching up and down a near-empty dance floor with a smoke machine belting out and bright lights. We paid to get in, so we were staying put, living in hope that it was going to fill up with lassies. It never happened. At the end of the night, we didn't have far to stagger, that was a bonus, and Paul had spotted a greasy spoon cafe just around the corner from our digs.

We overslept breakfast, there was only one choice left, the greasy spoon. We spent a fortune in the arcades before going to the Pleasure Beach. First thing we both bought were KISS ME QUICK hats. Paul was shitting himself to go on the Big Dipper, I was just scared of heights. It was far more dangerous going on the Grand National, where you had to mount a six-foot steel horse, it was a job and a half trying to get on the bloody thing, it was crazy when I think about the number of times I nearly fell off. We met Alec Finlayson from Tranent whilst going on the Revolution, which spun you up and around in circles, he also worked at Griggs. The Big Dipper was a doddle after that, we did it a couple of times. The American rollercoaster was the best laugh, finishing off on the Kentucky Derby, where you had to roll balls into holes to make your horse move, Paul was quite good at it, I was rank rotten.

We did a lot of walking that night after getting knocked back at every nightclub on the seafront 'til we finally ended up in the Galleon Bar. It was full of hardened Scottish drinkers, Paul had to carry me home. We were on our arse by Sunday, then came some good news, Mooney was in the money. He had his shirt on a horse that romped home at a good price, we were all set for Sunday night at the Gaiety Bar where all the east coast Scots would meet up, heaven forbid if we missed that night. The last night of our weekend and we were flush with cash thanks to Paul.

That night we marched into the Gaiety Bar, no questions asked. It was full of people we knew from East Lothian; Alec was there. Paul was getting the rounds in while Alec was trying to fire into a couple of lassies, he was at it all night, he wasn't budging for no one. I just sat there really quiet, sipping vodka and coke. Paul started chatting up her pal. By the end of the night, Paul told me the lassie Alec was chatting up fancied me, they wanted us to stay the night at their digs. Alec eventually moved away to let me in, she started chatting me up. I listened to her patter for a wee while but there was no way I was sharing a double bed with Mooney and two lassies, so I made way for Alec again.

"On ye go, Alec."

"They want the three of us to go."

"Nae chance."

It was a long walk home that night, I got the double bed to myself then realized I'd made a big mistake. Paul came back in the morning, eyes hanging out his head, constantly reminding me about what a great time he had, describing every last gory detail.

"You fucked up last night, Rainbow."

Back on the building site, Alec and Paul wound me up for weeks. Who in their right mind would pass up a chance like that, I must have been off my head. I wanted my first to be special.

Chapter 26

After receiving my provisional driving license through the post, I was on the lookout for a second-hand Vespa scooter, all my mates had their ears to the ground. It wasn't long before Paul McGuire came to my house telling me this guy called Grant McKenzie was selling a 100cc Vespa he had bought brand new. Grant had meticulously run his Vespa exactly to the manufacturer's handbook, gradually building up speed with reference to the mileage according to Paul.

"You should have a look at it, Rainbow, I'll take ye down."

Grant didn't live far; it was past the White House, so it was locally considered to be in the bottom Pans. We could see the scooter parked in his drive, it was maroon, had chrome bars fitted on the front, it looked the business. The good news was he hadn't sold it yet, he was still thinking about it, you could tell his heart wasn't in it to be a scooter boy anymore, he wanted a car. We hung about, talking for ages, I remember Grant was a good football player, and a decent guy at school. I could hardly take my eyes off the thing until he finally made me an offer, the price he asked for sent my heart racing, it was a steal, I felt like I was robbing him. We cemented the deal with a gentleman's handshake.

"You'll look after it, Rainbow?"

"Aye! I'll do that, Grant."

I'd meet up with Shep and Paul McGuire at the weekends, we'd go to Seton Sands camps. We'd usually go to the big hut where Kevin Morris was DJ until he had an almost fatal car crash down Longniddry Bents that left him in intensive care.

It was just another Friday night. I was cruising along through Port Seton behind a car that put its brake lights on. I thought it was heading for the garage on the left. As it was slowing up, I had almost overtaken the vehicle when it made a sharp turn right. My scooter hit the front driver's side, sending me careering up the pavement where my scooter crashed into a wall and launched me into the car park a fair distance. My chin acted as the brakes, my open-faced helmet flew off like a basketball.

Next thing I knew I was lying in a hospital bed next to Kevin Morris. Nurses kept waking me up every hour on the hour all through the night to ask me my name, date of birth and where I lived. I was in Ward 1, it was the brain ward. It was a pain in the arse getting woke up every hour, but the nurses had a job to do. I'd answered all their questions spot on every hour all through the night. In the morning, I just thought I could leave. I had to see the consultant doctor before I got any notion in my head. My chin was almost scraped to the bone, I was responding well though. The consultant came to see me, he was happy with my progress, it was down to me whether I wanted to stay in for another night. The nurses were urging me to stay but Saturday nights were always the best down the camps. It was a no-brainer, I was going to leave, the nurses were sad to see me go, they said I brightened up the ward. I was born in the connecting hospital –Simpson's Memorial.

I had to walk past Grey Friars Bobby, the Museum of Scotland, down to Waverley Station where I got a train home to the Pans. Rose told me Cookie had handed in my helmet; he witnessed the crash. I'd landed 20 feet into the car park, essentially, I'd missed a telegraph pole by inches, I was lucky to be alive. I still made the camps disco that night.

That car had killed my scooter, I was gutted when I saw the state it was in. Nothing could console me. I thought it was a write-off 'til Nigel and Johnny Grant came up to see me. They told me they could fix it for me. I thought they were winding me up, the scooter was mangled. Johnny asked me to pick two colors from a book. I picked an orange and red but they said it would be too much like Shep's, so I left it to them as I couldn't pick my nose.

A couple of weeks later, Johnny came to my door and handed me the keys back. "It's outside, Rainbow."

"You're joking!"

To my astonishment, the scooter looked even better than when I bought it. I don't know how they managed it. I was back in business, back on the road, and with a custom paint job. I wasn't too sure about the colours at first, but they grew on me. It looked like a brand-new scooter; it was two shades of green. I couldn't thank Johnny and Nigel enough; they were magicians in every sense of the word. I'll never forget what they kept telling me.

"You're an East Lothian Scooter Boy, we look after our own."

I drove up to a motorbike shop down Leith Walk in Edinburgh and bought second-hand black Belstaff full-face helmet. All these big bikes parked around the shop and my wee poxy scooter, more like a hairdryer on wheels compared to the beasts that surrounded it. I didn't have the black helmet long before Johnny took it, custom sprayed if East Lothian Scooter Club colors and it had my nickname on the front above the visor.

I was stripping asbestos from a tenement building down Easter Road with Ian Adams. I kept asking for a mask from Ian, he was too scared to confront Harry Grigg, so I confronted Harry. He gave me one secondhand paper mask. I only used it twice due to the buildup of snotters. He wouldn't give me any more. He told me if I wasn't happy, I could just get the bus home. I hated the taste of that asbestos – three landings we had to strip.

This job should have been for the laborers, it was unskilled, and they seemed to always have a multitude of face masks when you saw them. Ian Adams was a shite bag, too scared to put his foot down even when his health was at risk.

After we stripped the building of asbestos, we were to fit a less harmful fire-resistant sheet called Supalux, it was the new substitute for asbestos. I suggested to Ian we cut the Supalux with a handsaw so there would be fewer fine particles that hung in the air totally suspended, waiting for you to swallow a mouthful, which really hurt your throat. But Ian insisted we'd save more time using an electric saw. I was at Harry, asking for face masks, he sent me down the road. I was always back the next day, I was desperate to have a trade that much we stripped three floors of asbestos and fitted three floors of Supalux, Ian never said a word. He just got on with things as he always did.

With a custom scooter and custom full-face helmet, Shep and I drove the coast road all the way down to North Berwick and back like we were kings, obviously stopping off at the camps. Seton Sands was such a lovely place, I could see why people from Glasgow and Fife would jam-pack the place during summer holidays. We met a couple of older girls from Fife, they were fascinated with our scooters. When their boyfriends were away getting a carry-out, they invited us back to their caravan. We were real daredevils back then; I got a kiss before we got told to leave. Next time we met them, their boyfriends were on the way back from Fife, I got more than a kiss before we had to abandon ship. The girl really liked me, but we lived too far apart so that was it in a nutshell.

Had to get up really early in the morning for Scarborough because we were avoiding the motorway for everyone who didn't have full driving licenses. I strapped a sleeping bag on the back of my scooter. I put on as much clothes as possible under my fishtail parka. I decided not to stick L-plates on because the paint was still fresh and it looked amazing, it would taint the look of my custom paint job and just look plain silly. We were congregating with Clyde Valley Scooter Club at Tranent civic square. All around the square, right up the High Street, was buzzing with scooters. I turned to Shep. "This feels like *Quadrophenia*."

"It's amazing, Rainbow."

It was even better when the long trail of scooters started to leave the town heading for a turn off at Carberry near Whitecraig, where a long line of police was lying in wait. They must have had a tip-off; they were checking driving licenses. If you didn't have one on your person you received a five-day ticket to produce one at your nearest police station. The learner driver stickers never crossed my mind 'til the police were working their way towards me. I only had a provisional driving license in my wallet, I started to panic. I felt like doing a runner, but my scooter would be no match for a police car. Shep always told the truth.

"You're fucked, Rainbow."

I received a caution from the policeman and told to get a set of L-plates on ASAP. It broke my heart, but it could have been a lot worse. It may have conceivably destroyed the look of my scooter, but it was a result that I never got fined.

East Lothian Scooter Club and Clyde Valley were finally on their way. Johnny, Wilma and Muff were in the backup van behind us just in case anyone broke down. Avoiding the motorway added many hours to our journey. The 200cc led the way. Most of the time I just followed the procession. What a sight, seeing all the scooters travelling to a coastal town, just like the film I watched, you felt a sense of pride being part of it all. Then we hit an extremely steep hill, the gradient in degrees was 1 in 10. It was doing the rounds that if you make the top, you'll make it to Scarborough. I was passing 125cc, 150s even 200s on the accent. Most people were off their scooter, pushing it up the hill. My scooter had the smallest engine coming in at 100cc. Incredibly, I made it to the top without coming off. I had passed the 125s, I was now cruising with Colin Ferrier and the 150s. That wasn't good enough for me, I put the foot down and started tailing the 200s, I could see Nigel Grant. It was getting dark, next thing

I remember was looking up at Johnny Wilma and Muff. A chorus of voices were ringing in my ear.

"YOU ALL RIGHT, RAINBOW?"

I had fell asleep while driving, my scooter was 20 yards back down the road. Johnny and Muff lifted me into the van. They must have also lifted my scooter into the back of the van. Johnny started talking to me. "We were right behind you, Rainbow, you nearly hit a car. To think you'd drove all this way to crash one mile outside Scarborough."

All I could think about was if my scooter was okay. Muff reassured me. "It'll need a new exhaust but apart from that it looks fine and dandy, mate."

I truly suspected a case of ambiguity about what muff was telling me. Maybe he was just trying to put my mind at rest seeing as I didn't care about anything else. I still felt concussed after falling off my scooter, fell into a deep sleep. When we arrived in Scarborough, Johnny must have left me sleeping in the van while the boys put the tents up. I slept in the van all night. That sleep must have done me the world of good.

The scooters and van were parked right next to a funfair. We all thought it would be a good idea to go on this huge swinging boat that almost tipped you over the edge. We must have gone on it half a dozen times on the trot, I felt sick as a parrot. I went for a walk down the town with Shep and Doodle, we ended up buying tickets for an all-night Northern soul disco. We were the only ones in the scooter club that were up for it.

Muff took me to a spare parts market to find a new exhaust. He managed to get one that needed a bit of an adjustment, I never thought he would get it on, it was just a random part. It was chrome, it looked the fantastic, I was forever in his debt when he finally fitted the exhaust. it looked the business. You wouldn't think my scooter had been in a crash, Johnny's spray job was that good the scooter still looked minted. I took it for a run down the town just to try it out, it sounded better than ever. All my mates were waving to me, I kind of felt like the ace-face for a moment 'til I got flagged down by the police.

"Was I speeding, officer?"

"No, you've not got a helmet on."

I got away with another caution. All my mates were buckled over watching me push my scooter back up the hill.

Nigel always had the best scooter; Johnny could work miracles. He managed to get the front cover of The Who album, *The Kids Are Alright,* on Nigel's side panels. It was a picture of the band snuggled up under a huge Union Jack. Nigel loved Rangers so it was only fitting that his scooter was red, white and blue with his favorite band as the main focal point.

Everyone was hanging about the tent area with toothbrushes hanging out their mouths, Shep and I carried on the trend. We were talking to guys from all over Britain. It was hard enough for them to understand the Scottish accent never mind with a toothbrush hanging out your mouth.

It was the day of the all-nighter. Doodle had brought a suit with him, it didn't look crushed, he also had a pair of Oxford brogues. Shep and I stripped down to Fred Perry T-shirts, jeans and desert boots. They told me to bring my sleeping bag, once I got in the club, I realized what they meant. Everyone circled the dance floor, lounging on their sleeping bags when they were not dancing. Doodle declared to us, "I'm only going to dance to songs I know."

My philosophy was to dance when I felt like it because I'd never heard any of the tunes. We'd smuggled in bottles of juice to save us from drinking tap water in the toilet. I didn't feel tired all night but, in the morning, I was shattered. I was dreading the long drive home. I'd fell asleep on the way down, and that was after a good night's sleep.

I felt a bit shaky driving although I soon got my act together. The best part was going down the 1 in 10 gradient hills, I must have done in a set of brake pads. It was an amazing feeling successfully making it home to Prestonpans without falling off, a minor miracle considering the state I was in. I parked the scooter in the back garden then it was straight to bed.

Chapter 27

While waiting to get picked up in the morning for work, I was discussing last night's football with Jimmy, this was our only ever disagreement, it got a bit heated, he wasn't backing down, he had to get the last word, I had to threaten him to shut him up. It was no more than kid's stuff, playground stuff, handbags at five paces, Jimmy went in the cream puff, a huff that would last all the way to the yard. On arrival, he told his gaffer, George Grigg. I could see the three brothers, Harry, John and George circling. The Griggs hunted in a pack, I'd witnessed it the previous week when they all laid into Cameron, the apprentice plumber. Cameron was only looking for a lift to a job, God knows how he got there from Ormiston. The brothers Grigg laid into Cameron, he'd done nothing, the men done nothing, he was on his own, they kicked and punched the life out him, it was sickening. I felt bad for Cameron, I was too young to get involved, nobody spoke a word about the ordeal he suffered. I was on top of the van tying wood for Bobby Grant, the brothers Grigg were moving in for the kill, I could see it unfold before my eyes. George Grigg came up to the van where Bobby was handing up wood. "Get down here, son, I want a word."

I knew I would have to fight the three brothers; it was a carbon copy of what Cameron had to endure, but I'd fight back. I weighed up the situation, I thought I could take them, Cameron wasn't fighting back. I started to climb down the van. I'd never said a word to Bobby, he raised his voice. "You get back up there, son. And you FUCK OFF! Leave the laddie alone. That's us all done here, now BEAT IT!"

Bobby had a way with words, he had a way with people, he loved having a laugh, he could be loud, quiet as a mouse when grafting, he was one of the good guys. If Bobby hadn't intervened, I would have to fight the three brothers Grigg, all grown men, liberty-takers.

As soon as I'd got my provisional driving license, then a scooter, I applied to sit my motorcycle test, it took a while to fix a date. It was somewhere near West Barns, before East Fortune Market. I was hoping for signposts, I'd been down that way many times, never really gave it much thought, other than I'd find it or ask someone.

On the day of the motorcycle test, Rose told me to leave in plenty time, I was always late, she always reminded me I'd be late for my own funeral. I had to take a day off work, it was a fair distance, I allowed for an hour, I thought that was plenty, surely it couldn't be that hard to find. I set off to find the place, I had an hour. There were no signposts, nada. It was like looking for a needle in a haystack. I only came across one person, they directed me to a chicken farm. I went back on myself threw Drem, I went further east, near the market, up and down country roads, I almost gave up, 'til I saw a lone figure standing in a field. As I drove up the old farm road, I could see he was standing on a concrete area, I drove straight towards him.

"Is this where you sit your motorcycle test?"

"Yes, son. But you're ten minutes late."

"I'll be quick."

"It doesn't work like that, son."

"C'mon."

"Nope, rules are rules."

I felt gutted, no matter what I said about how hard it was to get here, in the middle of nowhere, he was having none of it. Maybe it was a blessing in disguise, maybe it was meant to be. I'd took a day off, waisted my time and lost the money I'd paid for the test. It was a bad day for me, I had to put it down to experience. I didn't learn anything, I was always late.

Leading up to the scooter rally in Southport I knew Paul's girlfriend, Catherine, had an empty house that weekend. Her mum and dad were going away, Paul was torn between her house and Southport. Paul has dodged Scarborough for similar reasons. I'd hung about with Shep most of the week cruising down the coast road. On the night before Portsmouth, Paul and I drove up to

Catherine's. The lovely Lesley Johnstone was at the front door with Catherine beckoning to come inside. We were a fair bit away from them when Paul turned to me. "What do you think, Rainbow?"

I fancied Lesley when I first walked her home from the Annex disco at 15. And at the labour club in Musselburgh when I was 16. It was a really tempting offer, a long weekend with a beautiful lassie. My mind was in overdrive 'til I remembered East Lothian Scooter Club were also doing the Blackpool pirate run on the Sunday. It was the September weekend, I revved my scooter and shot always from Catherine's house. I wasn't missing a scooter rally for anything, I never looked back.

Shep came to my house on the morning of Portsmouth run. Once again, we made our way to the civic square in Tranent where East Lothian Scooter Club met up with Clyde Valley Scooter Club. Once again, we were on our way, this time I was displaying learner plates front and back, but they were hardly noticeable where I had conveniently placed them, to show as much of my custom paint job as possible. I passed a few 100cc scooters that were in trouble by overheating. There was no doubt about it, Shep actually believed he was Jimmy the mod from the film *Quadrophenia*. We stopped a couple of times to discuss whether we just chanced it and took the motorway. We decided to keep to B-roads. It was amazing driving into Southport with all the light, all the scooters taking up the road. I drove in with Chops, this was his first rally, he was going berserk like a madman.

We parked the scooters, put up the tents and went for a pint at the nearest pub. We were not long in before a lassie was making herself known to me, batting the eyelashes and looking straight at me. Shep was on hand to give me some advice. "Go for it, Rainbow!"

I stood my ground, she came across with her pal, Chops was right in there. The lassie was all over me like bad rash. Nigel, Johnny, Muff and Shep were egging me on so I took her for a walk, Chops followed me with her mate. We walked along the seafront and sat on a bench. After a while, Chops was tapping my shoulder. I looked around; the bird was giving him a blow job. Suddenly it started to rain, we headed for the tents. After a wee while in the tents, I felt soaked to the bone. Thumping the back of the van I tried to get the lassie in, Johnny shouted out, "Just you, Rainbow."

I said goodbye and jumped into the back, trampling on heads, legs and private parts 'til I found a wee space to curl up. The next day we all thought it would be funny to buy a fake police hat. We didn't have them on long before Muff got strip-searched by the police right down to his underwear in the middle of the car park. We were all in fits of laughter, Muff never saw the funny side of it. His helmet got confiscated and we were told to take our fake hats off. Shep wanted to drive my scooter in a dirt track rally race.

"Fuck off! Drive your own scooter."

I bought a pair of yellow grips to cover my handles. You were meant to glue them and leave in a dry place for 48 hours, I left mine less than 12 in the soaking rain. The grips were slipping on the handles for months. It became difficult to make Blackpool on the Sunday. Southport was a wash out. We'd slept in the van for two nights.

We safely got to Blackpool and parked along from the Pleasure Beach. In the massive funfair, my dodgem broke down, so I started pushing it backwards, everyone was swerving to me, I was laughing my head off that much we all got kicked of the dodgems, the owner was going mental at us all. We were all standing at this punch ball that racked up points in accordance to how hard you'd hit it; everyone was egging me to have a go. I declined, Robert Peden jumped and pulled his trousers down, showing his bare arse, I got the message.

There was one good thing about Blackpool, the Gaiety Bar, that's were all the Scottish folk went. We were passing cans from a twenty-four pack. Everyone was still in our scooter boy gear, we kind of stood out from the crowd a wee bit. Everyone got smashed on beer that seemed to be never ending. This lassie was chatting to me while we were squeezed together on a balcony. She told me she worked in a shop at St James' Centre, I told her I was a joiner. She stayed close to me all night. Shep had a word in my ear. "You might get a hot bed, Rainbow."

The girl asked me to come back to her bed and breakfast. I was still a virgin; thought I had scored. We all left the bar that night singing, Nigel couldn't hold a tune. Muff was hanging onto everyone, he was steaming. I walked a great distance with the girl, it was quite creepy cutting through a venal past the car park. We got on really well, had a good laugh. We arrived at her digs; she'd lost the key so had to chap the sitting room window. Someone let us in, and we sat next to each other. I looked out of place in my army greens covered in scooter boy patches and a scooter rally T-shirt. I wasn't in there long before she struck up a conversation with a guy next to her who also worked in St James' Centre in Edinburgh. He was wearing decent clothes; I looked like a tramp and hadn't had a wash all weekend. Even although the girl kept telling me to stay, I felt that out of place I asked where the toilet was. I closed the living room door tightly behind me and quietly left through the front door making as little noise as I could. I walked all the way back to the van, started thumping it 'til they let me in. In the morning we made our way home. The rally was a disaster compared to Scarborough.

Chapter 28

We had booked the community centre for my 18th. The DJ was setting up and the labour club was setting up stall behind the bar. This guy walked in and went straight to the bar, I didn't know who he was, but he got a pint and just stood there. I had invited people by word of mouth so I guessed around 150 would attend. By the time the hall was full, it must have been closer to 300, half the pans had turned up, it was jam-packed, you could hardly move. I got a lot of cards and gifts from people who actually knew me, even Mandy Vanbeck, Tracy Allan, Pamela Brown and Diane Armitage from Tranent turned up. Everyone kept asking me what I wanted to drink.

"A fresh orange juice."

I was in training, the season was not finished, and I never drank alcohol anyway. I made a request to the DJ to play a Spandau Ballet song called 'Gold', I remember dancing to that song. I think most of the people who had been at Dukey's 18th just came along to mine. I did go over and say hello to Mandy, Tracy, Dianne, Pamela and their pals, and thanked them for coming. They did add a bit of colour to the party. I mostly stood with Rose, big Vic Shelley was the doorman, not that we needed one, he just offered to stand at the front doors. Another Spandau Ballet song, 'True', came on, I danced with Angela Gordon. The evening passed so quickly, before you knew it, I was back in the house, opening my presents. The night had passed so quick nothing really stood out in my mind except that I'm sure everyone enjoyed themselves. Rose had a wee glass of advocaat before I called it a night and went to bed.

The next day I woke up with an invigorating zest for life, put on Chalky White's steel toe caps and ran for 13 miles, holding a cold chisel in each hand passing by Wallyford, down to Levenhall in Musselburgh, along to the bottom Pans, continuing through Cockenzie and Port Seton, up the Dean Road past Longniddry and back along the long road to Prestonpans. It was literally the same distance and course as the Prestonpans half-marathon.

I won the Prestonpans half-marathon that year, setting a new course record. Considering I was using the toilet when the race began, I didn't do too bad. The organizers got me to kiss the gala queen. I also competed in the 26-mile Edinburgh marathon in 1986, I never won it but it was a good feeling going through the pain barrier around 17 miles and managing to sprint when I got sight of Meadowbank Stadium, one last lap around the track then I was over the line. I was the first person in my family to complete a full marathon.

I decided to visit Prestonpans Labour Club, I thought I could just walk in, but Gerald O'Brian asked to see my birth certificate, so I had to go home and get the document to prove I was 18. Gerald must have known I was borderline 18 because I went to school with his son, Kenny. He had to be sure, so he was only doing his job. He was a big committee man, Labour through and through. All I drank was fresh orange juice. It was funny seeing my mates falling about drunk and slavering a lot of pish. It was to become a weekly thing for me, so was the long run on a Sunday.

According to my friends, I was really old when I lost my virginity, I lost it to the same person who had a premonition way back at a disco in the British Legion, the same girl I was paired up with when I was picking potatoes. She was now a lady, she was beautiful, it was fate that brought us together. Who would have thought, all them years ago when we were kids, her premonition would come true. I didn't feel any different, I was already a man, I was eighteen. I knew a lot of friends had joined the army, some had got married, some had been tattooed, I lost my virginity to someone special, someone I'd met in Prestonpans British Legion as a kid. I also worked in the fields with her, that was the big deal to me.

Our relationship didn't last long, she dumped me for the singer in a band.

I'd been saving the pennies since I started work, never really went out, never had any bad habits, it was all going towards purchasing my first secondhand car, that was my way of thinking. I paid £400 for the scooter, sold it to Francis Burns for £300. He was delighted to take it off me. It was a cracking scooter, it had a tremendous engine, a fantastic paint job, it was in great condition, definitely worth every penny. Francis Burns had been asking me for a while to part with my scooter, he knew I was thinking about buying a car, his offers were going up every time I saw him. My savings were rising, his offers were rising, then we struck a deal. One last ride down the coast and the scooter was his.

Every night I checked the cars for sale in the local newspaper, *Evening News*. Eventually, I spotted two potential cars in the same street. Maria gave me a lift, we took Gerard McGuire, he was a mechanic. I was desperate to get a set of wheels, I was excited. It took us about twenty minutes to get to Milton Road, on the east side of Edinburgh. We arrived at the first house to see a stunning red Ford Capri Ghia, it was a T registration, looked immaculate, I wanted to buy it right there and then, it was minted. Gerard suggested we take a look at the Ford Escort, it was a year older, an S reg. The floor mats looked stinking, I didn't like the color, it gave me a horrible vibe, nothing attracted me to this car. Gerard kept going on and on about how easy it was to get parts for a Ford Escort, and it was cheaper insurance. Gerard put up a good case for the Escort, I had my heart set on the Capri. Reluctantly, I decided to go with what the trained mechanic said – I bought the older car, I bought the Ford Escort. The floor mats in the car were the type you had to wipe your feet on, on the street, on the way out.

For me to drive the car, I had to have someone who held a full driving license sitting beside me. Tombo had beat me to attain his full license, he was perfect for the job, we spent so much time together anyway, this was beneficial for me, he was the very man. It was different going down the coast in a car, even with the windows open. You could drive a lot faster; it was more dangerous. I'd paid for ten driving lessons from a guy in my street, he was a qualified driving instructor, well recommended, only took nine lessons and bought a car while waiting on my vehicle driving test.

I rarely went out, the odd birthday party now and again, drank lemonade, watched my pals falling about so drunk they could hardly walk. Tombo suggested we try a popular night club in Portobello, called Misty's. It seemed a reasonable idea, I'd just be drinking lemonade, Tombo said he'd only have a few drinks. This was music to my ears, it seemed like a perfect plan.

On the night we were going out, I got the chance to wear a pair of boots I'd bought that were not from the bottom Pans store – the rest of my attire was from there. I splashed on a ton of Paco Rabanne aftershave, it was for the ladies, it was really popular back in the 80s. Tam dressed almost the same as me, we were like twins, although he had jet-black hair. We said our goodbyes to Rose and Ed. Rose shouted, "Take care and mind what you're doing."

We were off, on an adventure of sorts, uncharacteristic of me, I'd never been to a nightclub. It took around twenty minutes to reach Misty's, Tombo showed me where to park, a short stroll and we were there, standing in the queue outside. We never got asked for identification, we walked straight through to the edge of the dance floor. Tombo begged the question.

"What are you having to drink?"

"Just a lemonade, pal."

I never danced in my life, I never danced at a disco, I never danced at the labour club, I wasn't a dancer. Tombo was scanning the dance floor for ladies to tap on the shoulder to dance. The ladies all danced in pairs, the guys had to pair up, tap the shoulder of the one they intended dancing with, they either danced with you or turned away. That was customary in 80s Scotland, it was an unwritten rule. Tombo was relentless at spotting potential females to dance with, I never had the guts to follow up. As the night passed, I summoned the courage to make a move, it wasn't like me, I felt like a different person. When the ladies turned away, it made you feel lower than a snake's belly, when they danced with you, it was magical, like you'd won the World Cup. I met Paddy Neilson, on the dance floor, we had the same boots on. I'd played football with Paddy, I was younger, he was older, he was a good player back then. He told me he'd signed for Heart of Midlothian FC, we really hit it off, we neighboured up as dancing partners. We had the same boots on, the music played on and on, we had a great laugh. Paddy knew all the ladies, we never got a knock back, no one turned away. Paddy had charm, he was a class act. I'd drunk so much lemonade; I had a great night. Tombo and I said our goodbyes to Paddy and left the club.

The weather had turned a bit blustery, it was also raining, quite heavy. While walking to the car Tombo suggested we drive to an all-night Chinese takeaway at the bottom of Leith Walk to try their spring rolls, he said they were great, I just went along with the idea. The windscreen wipers were going ten to the dozen, you could hardly see where you were going, I just followed the car in front and kept my distance. We came up to a set of traffic lights. When the lights went green for go, I followed the car in front, keeping a safe distance. Without using the indicator, the car in front braked hard, the movement of the vehicle suggested it was intending to turn right without indicating. I rammed on the brakes, the old second-hand car seemed to slide along the wet surface... BANG.

I'd smashed into the back of a police car. After a rapid inspection, my car seemed to be intact, no damage. The boot of the police car was fucked, it was a mess, the lock was holding it slightly ajar, like a wry, crooked smile. After putting my case forward to the officers, I did it all over again in the police station directly across the road. Tombo was cracking jokes, he looked drunk, the officers nearby arrested him. The station officer asked me if I'd been drinking.

"I don't drink alcohol, I'm a boxer."

"Okay, son."

I've no idea how Tombo made it out of there, everything seemed to be like a joke to him, I didn't find it funny, I had to have a word with him. Eventually we were on our way, thank God they saw it my way. We made it to the Chinese in Leith, it was closed. We got home safely; I made a remark to Tombo. "You were steaming tonight, eh!"

"So were you!"

"What do you mean?"

"I was putting a nip of vodka in every lemonade."

"I could have been done with drink-driving."

"You're okay."

"That's not the point, ya madman!"

I slept like a baby; it must have been the drink.

Chapter 29

On the day of my vehicle driving test, Maria's brother-in-law, Rob, offered to come with me as he held a full license and it was his day off. I drove to a cafe in Portobello, near the testing centre. I was a tad nervous drinking my coffee, this was my first attempt, I had to pass, I owned a car. The cafe was right on the corner of the eastern side of the promenade. It was a lovely wee cafe. I got the feeling it was now or never. I bought a bag of sweets on the way out. We got there early for a change; I was always late. The instructor followed me to my car, when he got inside, I offered him a sweetie, just to butter him up. He thanked me and asked whose car I was driving.

"It's mine, I bought it."

"You better pass your test then, son."

My confidence behind the wheel was overwhelming the nerves that seemed to disappear like mist on the windscreen as the heating kicked in. I drove around a few streets, indicating and stopping to give way to traffic. Then came the emergency stop, good job he had a seatbelt on, or he would have been thrown the windscreen. The streets were narrow, I had to demonstrate a three-point turn by reversing backwards into someone's driveway, this was the hardest part of the vehicle driving test. It seemed to go okay, I never crashed, but there was no way of knowing 'til I returned to the test centre.

"Raymond, I've scored you on a points system, and would like to congratulate you on passing your driving test."

"Thanks so much, please help yourself to another sweetie."

Harry Grigg asked me if I'd like to go to college for joinery. It was a no-brainer, anything that could further my education of my profession would be welcome, it would give me a break from lifting bags of rubbish down three flights of tenement stairs. I was to attend Esk Valley College in Dalkeith; it couldn't happen quick enough. The real reason G Grigg & Sons first sent their apprentices to college was because Harry's son, Stephen, was being sent to learn plumbing, it was fortunate for the apprentice joiners that year, it was a landmark year in the history of the firm. This was an opportunity to achieve a formal certificate by way of City & Guilds in carpentry and joinery. It was a two-year course, seeing as we only had one year of our apprenticeship to go, we only had one year to pass the exams, and complete the tasks we were given in the workshop.

Every Friday you'd get an hour for your lunch, some guys would go to the pub, some would sit in the canteen, I would go to visit Maria, who lived a few miles away in Bonnyrigg. Maria made me a bite to eat, we got time for a wee catch-up, then I was back to college, like a flash. There was a guy in my class I went to school with called Archie, we went home the same road, we raced all the way. It was a very dangerous road, we were young, Archie's car was brand new, I had an old banger. The only way I could win the race was taking serious, life-threatening, daredevil maneuvers that were so outrageous, your life flashed before your eyes. I would overtake Archie on blind corners, when I look back, it was stupidity. I didn't care, I had no care in the world, I had to have a considerable lead before we hit the straight part of the road leading to Whitecraig. I mostly got the better of Archie, in my old banger, he thought it was madness, I totally agreed with him, I honestly don't know how I made it home alive every Friday.

On my way to Esk Valley College, the rain was pissing down. I passed Francis Burns riding my old scooter, he could hardly see where he was going, I was sitting inside my car with the heating on full blast, I gave Francis a wave.

Dukey chapped my door one night. He told me he had been dating this girl from the Pans called Audrey Cunningham and he had been sitting in her house talking to Audrey and her pal, Paula Ramage. He had told them I was his cousin and a boxer and that I was single. They had asked him to describe me, Paula said she could remember me from the year before at Port Seton swimming pool. She remembered I was the whitest boy there, white as a sheet and I wore red, white and blue hooped swimming shorts, and I had short blonde hair.

"That's some memory she's got, Dukey."

"That's no' it all. She fancy's you and I've arranged a blind date for this Friday above the pond hall, it's a Valentines disco for Benji's football team."

I thought Dukey was off his head. Paula Ramage was the best-looking girl going about. All I did was work, train, fight and sleep. I thought I was dreaming; the alarm was going to wake me up any minute for work. But Dukey was sitting there insisting I had a blind date this Friday.

It was a good night for February, I just wore the jeans and T-shirt I'd got from the co-operative store down the bottom Pans. Rose would save up money on a club card and once it was full, she would let me pick what I wanted to wear. I wore Brutus jeans, desert boots and a Fred Perry, and a wee dash of Eddie's Old Spice on the cheeks.

We walked to the pond hall with George Montgomery. He was telling us that the best-looking lassie he had seen was Claire Sword from Musselburgh. Dukey had to stop him there and point out Claire was my cousin but told him to wait 'til he saw Paula. I just let them debate away, I still didn't believe that I was meant to be going on a blind date with Paula. The previous summer nobody in the pool could take their eyes off her. What a tan she had; she was tall with long blonde hair. I still didn't believe she was wanted to meet me. I was so nervous.

We arrived at the disco and there was no sign of Paula. I was drinking fresh orange juice as per usual. The bands were playing, still no sign of her. Stuart McDonald commented he hadn't seen me in a long time, he thought I was boxing, and why was I out tonight. Stuart was a lead singer in a band, he wore cool clothes, he was good-looking and had no trouble pulling a girl. A girl once left me for him. Dukey stepped in... "He's here for a date with Paula Ramage."

"No way, man, she's going to be mine, I've watched her grow up," said Stu.

"Well, we'll wait and see then, eh?"

Dukey seemed confident the date was still on but as the time passed, I grew wary that he had just spun a lie to get me out the house. Now I was more nervous that Stuart wanted her.

I just stood there talking to pals I hadn't seen for a while, keeping one eye on the door, thinking, dreaming, believing Paula would just walk in. I began to give up hope. I told Dukey I was going home; she wasn't coming, and I was feeling sick with all the fresh orange. He tried to reassure me she'd be here. I was almost ready to walk out when this tall blonde wearing a smart designer dress came walking through the door like Bo Derek from the film, *10*. I was gobsmacked, she walked over to a table on the other side of the hall. Stuart McDonald said, "She's mine!"

Dukey said, "No chance, pal."

I was confused. My heart was going ten to the dozen. I kept saying to myself, *why would Paula pick me?* She could get anyone she wanted. She looked amazing.

Dukey said, "Come over with me." I wouldn't go, I totally froze. I wasn't going anywhere. He went across the hall and sat chatting to them. After a while, he came back and said, "She wants to meet you."

"Am no' gone over there."

"C'mon, you'll be fine!" I was shitting myself. The Duke said, "Follow me!"

Hesitantly I began to edge forward. Dukey was at their table before I was halfway there. Leaving the bar area was a start so I made a bold effort to keep going until I reached the table. Dukey instructed me to sit next to Paula. I was in deep shit now, I didn't know what to say, I was so shy. She was so beautiful, she turned around and said, "Hiya, Raymond."

I felt myself starting to choke, my throat was dry, I had heartburn from all the fresh orange. Panic mode was quickly setting in.

"Hiya."

"Would you like to dance?"

"A cannae dance."

"C'mon, you'll be fine."

Paula stood up and walked onto the dance floor, beckoning me with a hand gesture. I was useless at dancing; knew I'd make a right fool of myself. I stood up and shuffled towards her. This was harder than getting in the boxing ring. I could feel my face burning, my feet could hardly move. I danced a bit like Herman Munster from *The Adams Family*, just sort of swaying from side to side.

"I'm sorry I was so late, I was at work, I'm a hairdresser."

"I'm a joiner."

I knew I was embarassing myself, but she didn't seem too bothered. Then a slow dance came on, and we knew it was near the end of the night. She put her arms around, so I did the same. I felt like a million dollars, king of the castle. You only had to sway from side to side, I knew how to do that. When the song finished, we returned to our seats. I could not talk much about anything apart from boxing, so I just sat there quiet as a mouse as she told me all about her job. After the last song she asked me if I'd walk her home.

We made our way out the pond hall, it seemed very straightforward, in reality, my nerves were shaking. It felt like a dream, I'd fancied Paula from the moment I laid eyes on her, and now I was walking her home. She was so cool, hip and trendy. On the other hand, I dressed in the best I could find using Rose's co-operative store club card. We were like chalk and cheese, we both had blonde hair though. It was amazing just walking beside her. I could smell her distinct perfume that she was constantly using, it smelt beautiful, it seemed to linger in the cool breeze. Walking up Fishers Road and into her street, it was there our lips would meet. She leaned forward and gave me a peck on the lips. While I was recovering my head from the clouds, she had written her phone number.

"Thanks for walking me home."

"You're welcome."

I almost floated home. It was a long way back to my house, but it didn't matter a jot. I had Paula's phone number; I had the whole world in my hands. All I had to do was give her a call.

We arranged to meet the following Saturday. I met her at the bus stop in the bottom Pans, just down from Coffin Lane. Coffin Lane was a narrow path with high walls separating the graveyard from Lowe's field. Polwarth Terrace to Coffin Lane was almost a straight line that took you to the bus service that operated the coastal route. I was five minutes early; she was bang on time.

After introducing Paula to Rose and Ed, we finally spent some time together listening to music, watching telly, we had a laugh. Although our fashion sense was miles apart, we got on like a house on fire, really hit it off, big time.

We held hands all the way to the bus stop where she arrived, this way we could see her bus coming.

As she let go to catch her bus on the other side of the road, I summoned the courage.

"What are you doing for the next 50 years?"

"What do you mean?"

"Will you be my girlfriend?"

"Yes."

Chapter 30

Haddington Amateur Boxing Club went to see Scotland versus Canada to watch our club heavyweight, John Brown, fight. I was more interested in a light middleweight from Irvine, in Ayrshire, called Alec Mullen, he made it look so easy, I couldn't take my eyes of him for a second.

After training on Tuesday night, Hamish told me I was fighting another Zetland ABC boxer called Iain Cameron on Friday night in Edinburgh. He was an Eastern District champion and he'd fought for Scotland. I was still a novice, but I trusted Hamish.

At work I told Bobby and Hector, they were always full of encouragement. I'd never read a book in my life, all my book reports at school were written from the synopsis as you opened the front cover. I'd had Hector's book for months; it was about a boxer called Freddie Mills. I was a really slow reader, nobody in my house ever helped me read. I had eventually caved in and flicked to the end of the book to find out Freddie Mills got shot. At dinner time I gave the book back.

"Did you enjoy it, son."

"Aye, it was great."

We were all sitting on bags of plaster eating our sandwiches, the fine dust from the plaster spoiled the taste. Hector told me the great Joe Louis would catch flies to sharpen up his jab. Immediately I stalked a fly like a tiger throwing out my left jab around the room, there was no way I was giving up. Eventually I caught the fly, Hector was impressed.

"You've got a rapier-like quick jab just like your dad, son."

On a Friday I went to college. I'd race Archie home every week. My old Escort was no match for his brand-new Astra, so I had to be a daredevil when it came to be taking blind corners. The road home was narrow and had more bends than the Monaco Grand Prix. Archie took a quick lead; I was playing catch up most of the way, stuck behind two other cars. A total blind corner was coming up, I dropped down the gears and flew into the opposite lane glancing over at Archie as I passed him, it was the shock on his face that got me. It was madness overtaking three cars at a blind corner. I was young and stupid, the adrenaline that was pumping through my veins that day was through the roof. To beat Archie, I had to take chances with my life and others because there was no way my old banger was beating him on the straight. Most of the time, I beat Archie by driving like a lunatic, I hated getting beaten. Looking back, I would never do such foolish acts of sheer madness.

On the way to the fight I was buzzing, I couldn't contain myself, my confidence level was through the roof with excitement. I was really looking forward to getting into the boxing ring. I'd never felt this way since I was with Bob Scally, and Alec Kelly taught me.

The scene was an industrial club in Gorgie. There wasn't much room to warm up, I mostly spent my time wrapping my hands and getting my kit on. Hamish called me. "You're next up, Raymond."

I was nervous but the excitement took over. There was no raised floor, the boxing ring was on the concrete. The bell sounded for round one. I danced back and forth swaying my hands from side to side, something Bob taught me. Iain was teeing me up for the big right hand, but I had him puzzled with my movement. Stepping in and out, then away, was my strategy. I could tell he was a fine boxer by the way he carried himself. I felt that fit I never even sat down during rounds. I was coming at Iain from all angles, he must have thought he was surrounded. Straight jabs were glancing by my head. I kept to the game plan, step in, step out, move away, and kept shaking my hands from side to side. I stuck to the jab and never got involved. After three rounds, Hamish said to me, "The Commonwealth Games."

I never paid much attention to him. I got my arm raised on a majority decision. Owen Smith introduced himself, I'd followed him since I was a kid. He said in the changing rooms, "You might get the best boxer award, you fought really well."

I never thought much of that either because it was an away show. It was good to finally meet Owen. We never had much time to talk, I knew he was my dad's protege. There was lots I wanted to say to him. However, Hamish gathered the troops together and we were off, never even stayed 'til the end of the show.

All the boys at work were over the moon. Bobby sent me to work with Peter Hill. I found him tiling a shower under a great puff of cigar smoke. Peter was funny, he would argue that the grass was blue. He was a lifelong Rangers fan. I learnt how to tile a bathroom. I hated any kind of smoke, but the banter was cracking. He always wore overalls, so Maria bought me a brand new pair. They were blue, obviously Peter thought they looked smart. He sent me to do a job for the plumber, Tam Lamont. I was to fit a new door up a set of ladders. Tam was using a blowtorch on a copper pipe while I made my way up the ladder. As I was nearing to top, I smelt something burning. Tam had set fire to my new boiler suit. I jumped off the ladder, Tam was rolling me about on the ground throwing over coats.

"That's it, Raymond, keep rolling."

"Fuck you, ya cunt."

Tam had set alight my boiler suit with his blow torch, the flames almost singed my hair. What a laugh we had about it, but that was the end of the boiler suit.

At training, Hamish told me Iain Cameron from Zetland wanted a rematch. Two weeks to the day, Haddington had a home show at the labour club in Tranent. That was to be the venue – that was to be the rematch. Tam Lamont took 40 tickets off me, that's not counting the tickets I sold myself. I heard the Terry Wiles bus to Tranent was rocking, a lot of punters made their way by foot across the bing and up Church Street. The whole of the back in the labour club was full of Panners singing, "HERE WE GO, HERE WE GO, HERE WE GO!"

They were all steaming before they got there. It was a long night. It had the most bouts I'd ever seen on a show, I was second top of the bill. After watching the first half of the show I decided to get ready to fight. My opponent, Iain Cameron, was almost ready, doing some warming-up exercises. I just took my time, remembering to tie the gold tassel my dad won at the European Games on my left leg. I had got 'RAY' printed on my shorts, also on my lead leg. It was the first time I felt confident to wear it in my 14th fight. I only lost once on points in Perth, I got robbed that night. This was my homecoming fight in front of a hall full of Panners who were now dancing on the tables. My fight was next, I felt butterflies but confident. Marching into the hall was something else.

"HERE WE GO, HERE WE GO, HERE WE GO!"

Hamish said to me, "You've got more followers than Geronimo."

As I looked down the hall there was a sea of Panners on tables and chairs, roaring their lungs out. There was no way of getting them to sit down, there would have been a battle that would have ended the show, they were not bothering anyone. The pressure was on, I had to make this the fight of my life. Iain Cameron must have thought he was walking into a hostile foreign country. Iain was tall and rangy, he had height and reach advantage, so I just adopted the same tactics as two weeks ago. I was stepping in and out, swaying my hands from side to side, while moving my head. I wasn't giving him a target to focus on while piling up the points with measured jabs that were finding the target.

Hamish told me to go for him in the second round. I did manage to knock Iain through the ropes that brought about a standing count, I never followed up, just went back to boxing. One round to go, the crowd were going mental. All I had to do was stay on my feet. I showed better feet-work that night than Kenny Buchanan. It was my finest performance; I'd reached the pinnacle of what I had set out to achieve as a wee boy wearing a caliper dreaming of stepping through the ropes. My name was called out as the winner by unanimous decision this time. I shook hands with Iain for the last time. He never wanted another rematch.

I took the trophy down to show the Panners and stayed with them 'til my name got called out as best boxer of the night. This time the trophy was a huge cup, the Panners filled it with strong alcohol, they made me take a drink. Hamish's daughter asked me to give this lassie a kiss but I'd started seeing Paula so I had to decline her offer as nice as I could. Iain Cameron was in the dressing room; I shook his hand again and thanked him for the fight. When I'd got changed, the Panners were still in the hall, singing their wee hearts out. I left my trophies with them; you could imagine it took a long time to clear the hall that night.

Chapter 31

Harry Grigg said my time was up, I'd finished my apprenticeship, he was letting me go. I was the only apprentice to pass my City & Guilds in carpentry and joinery. I was the first to achieve this acclamation in the history of the company, and the only apprentice to get paid off that year.

I had to travel to Granton, on the west side of Edinburgh, to find work. It was a fair distance from Prestonpans, driving through the city in rush hour traffic. You had to clock in using a card machine that punched a hole exactly on time. Sometimes the clock was well fast, if you were adjudged to have clocked in a minute after 8am, the company docked your wages – your pay would be less than expected at the end of the week. I was borderline every morning, on account of the distance I traveled, through numerous traffic lights. The sheer volume of traffic at that time of the morning was a nightmare.

One morning a car pulled up at amber, just as the traffic light was tuning to red. The car was almost through the lights leading from Musselburgh to Joppa. I rammed on the brakes, there was a slight collision, ever so slight. The driver jumped out in a rage, shouting obscenities. I reversed a tiny bit, got out my car, trying to explain my case. There was no damage to either car, the guy started shaking his fist at me, he was a big man, trying his best to intimidate me. I got that worked up, I started yelling back at him. I heard a shout, "Hook him, Rainbow!"

The call was insinuating I punch this overly aggressive stranger. I was standing so close to the guy, right in his face, not giving an inch. By this time, everyone in the queue was peeping their horns, the lights were at green to go. I just stood there as the big fella walked back to his vehicle, shouting his mouth off. The traffic lights were back to red, it was a game of cat and mouse most of the way, the guy drove very slowly to piss me off, I got my wages docked by half an hour that day, I didn't clock in 'til just after 8:15am. The clock machine could have been wrong, I wasn't going to argue, I just took my medicine, took it on the chin.

I was assigned to work as a finishing joiner, in England it was known as second fix. I was the person who fitted doors, facings, skirting, anywhere left that you could see. There lay my first problem. The doors were literally plywood with a corrugated cardboard inner, I never knew about the wooden inner that was to accommodate the latch, the part that closed the door. I'd fitted half my doors wrong; I wasn't sure what to do, I threw them in the skip, acquired new doors from another flat in the tenement. These mistakes kept happening over and over, I was improving, but when I was spotted by the foreman carrying doors around the corner of the block, that was the last straw. He instructed me to collect my tools, that he was taking me somewhere. I feared the worst.

On the way to the office, I was getting some stick from the general labourers in the back of the van. I took everything with a pinch of salt, I embraced myself for the inevitable. To my astonishment they'd partnered me up with a guy called Tony Clarke, we were to work as roughing joiners – first fix joinery. Tony was intriguing, intelligent and a genuinely nice person to be around, he always told the truth. I admired him; he was someone I aspired to become on a building site. His manners was pleasant, his wit was well beyond his years, a proper gentleman. Tony and I just seemed to gel. He did self-defense –martial arts were the way he expressed himself, he went to big conferences held by Dan Inosanto, the legend Bruce Lee's training partner.

Aided by Tony's close friend and fellow Edinburgh man, Rick Young, he was going to the United States of America that summer to meet Inosanto. It was fascinating how passionate Tony was about martial arts. He gave me a book about Bruce Lee, I felt too embarrassed to say my reading was so poor that I'd never be able to read the book, I mostly just studied the pictures. Tony was a bit older than me, I always respected my elders, no matter if it was only a few years. He was a seasoned campaigner in this game, his methods were well explained over a cup of tea and a sandwich at break time, I followed everything he said, and we became a strong partnership.

There was a couple of joiners working in the flat next to us, one of them was from the Pans, his name was John Reilly. He had been getting up early doors to catch buses to work, I offered to give him a lift. I had never met John before, he was around ten years older, he was from the bottom Pans. John spoke to me all the way to Granton, I was quiet, still a bit shy, had to concentrate on the road first and foremost. According to what he said, he enjoyed treating his family to an Indian takeaway, his favorite meal was rogan josh, he had my mouth salivating the way he described the contents.

One day we stopped near the office to clock in, that was the last time I managed to start the car. It was a cheap second-hand motor, you only get what you pay for, I only paid what I could afford. Gerrard McGuire had thoroughly inspected the car when I paid cash for it, maybe it was the crash, maybe it was just bad luck, you only get what you pay for in life. I always paid in hard-earned cash, I always paid for everything I owned.

Next to The Lady Susan pub in the bottom Pans was a car dealership on the corner, I perused the cars at night when it was closed and did the same on Saturday morning. This guy came up to me and introduced himself as Noel. He said he'd take care of me, he said I could get a car on finance. This meant sticking myself in debt, I was at the mercy of Noel's trust, his integrity, his dealership. After negotiating a deal, I was off in another old second-hand car, ladened with debt. I felt a wee bit uncomfortable, but I was back on the road, it made getting to work a lot easier.

Maria was giving thought about moving to Leeds, in England. She promised me that she would give me her car when she received a company car. Her car had only done several thousand miles, I was gutted she was considering moving, we had only just begun a proper friendship, having transport gave me more opportunities to visit. Paula and I would regularly visit, we even stayed overnight once.

When visiting Paula's house, there was an idyllic charm about the place. She had a big brother, mother, father and her own room, everything felt right, I sensed normality. This was something I couldn't get my head around, they even bought their food from Marks & Spencer. It all seemed perfect, they were perfect. Paula showed me how to do the washing up quickly, grabbing plates and cutlery, clean with Fairy Liquid, then straight on the rack next to the sink to dry, no dishcloth required. It was fascinating seeing how much they cared for each other, it was fascinating seeing how close they were, it was a privilege to be accepted into such a lovely family. Paula's brother, Derek, was cool, he was easy to talk to. Her dad, Jim, was everything you could expect to be in a father, her mother, Maurine, was just like Paula, so loving, so caring, so infatuated with buying clothes.

It became like a home from home for me. I trusted them 100%, I always found it hard to trust, it was easy with Paula's family, they made me feel like one of them, I felt elated in their company. Having my tea there was like dining out compared to Rose's watery stew. There was one thing I noticed very quickly about food from Marks & Spencer – there was no waste, everything got ate, clean the plate, put in the rack.

One evening, Maurine and Jim had their friends over for a game of Trivial Pursuit, they were all having a drink, their friends were half cut with the alcohol, especially the lady. They asked Paula and I to play, we all got paired up, I was paired with the lady who was a bit tipsy, she was answering most of the questions for us. I needed the toilet; Maurine stopped the game 'til I returned. The lady who had obviously drunk too much expressed, "Why did you stop the game? He's not going to know the answer, he's a boxer."

The question was about science, it seemed a long shot, maybe the lady was right, they may have saved a few minutes, I might not have a clue. Maurine asked the question, I nailed it straight away, my answer was correct. In other words, you should never judge or underestimate a person. I was underestimated, I was judged, the lady was drunk, I didn't care. It was like being the underdog all over again, I devoured the moment in self-gratification.

Sometime after New Year, I met Maria. She had something to tell me regarding Rob, she was desperate to tell me, she said she was shocked, she swore me to secrecy, she said it was a big deal. I knew what she was going to say, so I got there first.

"Rob's gay?"

"How did you know, Raymond?"

"He could never give me any advice about girls, it was just a guess."

"Who do you think his partner is?"

"The minister, Bill."

"How did you know, Raymond?"

"It's obvious, they run the Boys' Brigade"

Maria looked a bit worried, she produced photos of Alan dressed up as a ladyboy, caked in make-up, bright red lipstick, scantily dressed. Rob was a professional photographer. She asked me what to do.

"If you're worried, take Alan out the BBs, I think he'll be okay, Rob's not going to touch his nephew."

"I'm taking him out, Raymond, the pictures freak me out."

"There's your answer."

Chapter 32

It was great to see Tony again, he'd been on holiday to the United States of America. He'd been to martial arts conventions, he'd brought back new music for the ghetto blaster. There was one song in particular that stuck in my head, 'Saving All My Love for You', it was a slow number, I kept singing that song over and over. Tony made me a tape of an album called *Whitney Houston*. I'd never heard of her, he told me she was big in the USA, this was her debut album, I could not get that ballad out my head, even Paula was impressed.

Tony and I got moved on to finishings – secon fix joinery. Fitting doors became my specialty, between us, we had a system. It got cold on the building site in winter, wearing lots of clothes, cotton gloves without fingers, cotton bonnet, Tony had one that covered your ears. With the two of us working hard, we could stop for a cup of coffee and a sandwich before the cold eventually crept up, then you felt a slight shiver, it was time to get back on the tools, regenerate some heat in your body.

Tony wanted to watch me box in the Eastern District Championships, he was kind of local to that area, it was pay at the door, it wasn't like a show, this was business. I was facing Jim Forbes in the semifinals, I was more interested in saving my energy for the final. I went through the motions without really breaking sweat, I made a big mistake, I totally underestimated Jim, he won on points. I congratulated him and wished him all the best. Climbing down the steps of the boxing ring, I spotted Tony, I headed straight to him.

"You're fitter than that, Raymond."

"I know, Tony."

"Promise me you won't do that in the Scottish."

"Honestly! I promise."

My dad told me to meet him in the North British pub at the foot of the walk in Leith after work. I was working in Granton, so it was easy enough to get there. I was more worried about parking my car in Duke Street than the fight itself. It was hard to find because there was not a sign outside, I had to ask someone. It looked like a rough pub with local punters who were quite frankly off their head. I told the barman I was to meet my dad in here. He was very pleasant, introduced himself as Harry Anderson. My dad was running late so I ordered a fresh orange. I turned to this big fella standing next to me and asked him a question.

"Is someone sitting there?"

He picked up the jacket on the chair and hurled it over his shoulder into a small booth full of seats. "Naw, son, I'm Danny Gallagher!"

We shook hands and I sat down. Harry told me he played striker in the German Bundesliga. I made a remark that the ceilings were very high. Harry told me a guy who came in there called Jimmy Pace could run up the wall and touch the cornice, he was a European champion at karate. I nursed that fresh orange like you wouldn't believe. Harry asked me who I was waiting on, once I told him we had a great crack. I felt comfortable speaking to him, told him half my life story. He said I should write a book. When my dad eventually appeared, I was munching on an apple.

"What are you eating that for, son?"

'I'm hungry.'

"It will just upset your stomach, we're boxing shortly."

My dad was having a blether with Harry, big Danny was shouting the odds at anyone, even having an argument with himself.

We left the North British and headed for Sparta in McDonald Road near the top of Leith Walk. My dad insisted we weighed in. He weighed 10st 5lbs, I tipped the scales at 10st 7lbs, there was only two pounds difference. Ironically, we were actually in the same weight division at professional level.

I reminded him of our agreement. "If I beat you, you won't fight again."

"And if I win, you'll stop boxing."

My dad and I walked into the ring to the tune of Gerry and the Pacemakers' 'You'll Never Walk Alone'.

We shook hands. He said to me he'd be impressed if I lasted three rounds. I retorted by claiming I'd do as many rounds as it took. As we entered the world-famous boxing ring, my dad turned to me. "Remember, I'm the referee."

"Aye, okay, Dad."

We went to our respective corners. I was in the far away corner looking down the hall at paintings of my dad and grandad when he won the world title, my dad was in the home corner nearest the changing rooms. We came out and touched gloves. It was like fighting a ghost. He peppered me with jabs that were coming from nowhere. All I could do was stand and dance around, parrying where I could. It was more of the same in the second, I was mostly on the defensive. He was standing on one side of me, and I could clearly see him, in a fraction of a second, he had scored a shot and was on the other side. His body of work was out of this world, but I was determined to stay focused, determined to stay in the fight. I was fighting a ghost in the third round as well. I started to get frustrated, attempting to catch him with a good shot. In the fourth I started landing some jabs of my own. I was constantly trying to tee him up for the left hook. Some of the rounds were lasting up to six minutes, I tried to point this out to him.

"Dad! That round lasted six minutes."

"I'm the referee."

The longer the fight was going, the closer I was getting to landing my big left hook. In the ninth round, I almost caught him flush with a beauty while piling up the points. It seemed to me the longer this went on, the more chance I had of catching him square on with a big left hook. After the tenth, I was standing in my corner with my back to my dad, looking at the famous paintings on the wall when he surprised me by throwing his arms around me.

"You've got what it takes, son."

My dad was crying with tears of joy. That's all I ever wanted to hear in my life. A living legend and father telling me I had what it takes...

I'd just shared the same ring as an undisputed world champion. In the dressing room, while we were getting changed, my dad said, "You'd make a good club fighter and get a shot at the British title; the rest is up to you, son."

That was more than enough for me. I was so happy to make my dad proud of me. He respected me as a boxer.

"You'd be more suited to the professional game, son."

I had only been boxing for two years. This was music to my ears. I'd never considered turning pro. It was that far away from my mind, it was never on the radar. All I ever wanted to hear since I put on a pair of boxing gloves was the words 'you have what it takes'. Hearing this from my lifelong hero was so exhilarating. I was now floating on air with the sound of the words my dad spoke. My dad never fought another unlicensed fight in his life again.

Chapter 33

It was almost the end of training one Tuesday when a call came from Edinburgh, it was the famous Sparta Boxing Club. Their most experienced boxer, Owen Smith, was requesting a fight with our most experienced boxer, Ian Krawiec. Ian point-blank refused the fight. Hamish returned to his office, asking me the question, "Will you take the fight, Raymond?"

"Aye."

Having had less than fifteen fights, I was still considered a novice class fighter, Owen and Ian were open class, meaning they could fight anyone. I was surprised to be asked to take the fight, taking into account I left Sparta to fight for Haddington ABC.

When I was growing up, I would only read the boxing section of local paper, *Evening News*. I had followed Owen's progress over the years with headlines such as 'Sparta Powerhouse Owen Smith', and, 'Ken Buchanan Prodigy, Owen Smith'. My second fight was on the undercard, in the first half of the show, where Owen topped the bill in the second half, when I fought for Sparta. This was a step up in class for me, I'd been racking up an unbeaten run, I was confident, and Hamish knew that. This was my time, my chance to open many eyes in the Scottish boxing fraternity. I finished off my workout in the same fashion Bob Scally had taught me.

That night after training, I gave fellow clubmate, Mark Logan, a lift to Port Seton in my car. The weather was abysmal, heavy rain and strong winds swirling the air. I was really excited, couldn't contain myself. While driving like a man possessed, Mark fastened his seat belt. Seat belts weren't mandatory back then – that was a sure sign of no confidence in the driver. I was driving like Nigel Mansell; my old banger replaced his Formula One car. Every bend in the road, I almost lost control, it didn't stop me from pressing my foot on the gas. I could tell Mark was shitting himself, he was stuck to the seat, with a look of fear. This was different from climbing through the ropes, this was madness. I disrespected the weather conditions; I disrespected my ability. We had to negotiate one extremely tricky s-bend at the top of Fishers Road. All I had to do was ease my foot off the gas. Going into the first corner, I ploughed my foot through the accelerator, we started spinning around in circles, I totally lost control, then, BANG! I looked over, Mark's trousers were wet near the crotch area, his face was a picture of shock. He mustered the words, "Are we dead, Rainbow?"

"Naw! We're still alive, pal."

It was blowing a gale force wind, with rain falling like the heavens had burst. I got out my car to inspect the damage. I'd hit an old stone dyke around the first bend with the rear of my car, it was really dark, feeling with my hands and from what I could see, the car was relatively unmarked from what I could tell. I turned the ignition on, everything seemed to be okay, I was facing the way I came. After a few maneuvers, we were on our way again. I dropped Mark off at the bottom of Fishers Road, he got out the car, then leaned back in to have a word.

"Remember me no' to ask you for a lift again, that was mental, Rainbow."

Mark was just having a laugh, but he never asked me for a lift again in his life.

The show was the day after training, relatively short notice. My granda wanted to watch me fight Owen, he drove down from Musselburgh to pick me up. The show was in Edinburgh, at the Thistle Foundation, it was in a complex where all the residents were handicapped or disabled, the show was set up as a fundraiser for charity. On the way to the venue, I could never tell where Niddrie ended and Craigmillar began, our destination was close to that line. I felt strong as an ox, a natural welterweight, I had all the tools in the box, and was more than ready to unleash my weapons of mass destruction. This was my time.

Hamish handed me a programme and pointed out Owen and I were top of the bill, not too bad for a mere novice. This was a big show, boxers had traveled as far as Aberdeen, and further beyond. I watched the first half of the show before getting prepared. I went through my usual drill, tying a ribbon with gold tassel around the calf of my lead leg. It was all that remained of a teddy bear I was given as a child, it was a present that was secretly given to me by my dad, he had won it at the European Championships. I remember ripping the eyes out, I remember ripping it to shreds, all that was left intact was the ribbon and tassel.

I was ready, lying down, relaxing, with my feet up on a small chair to let all the lactic acid dissipate. After a short amount of time, Hamish alerted me Owen was refusing to fight unless he got paid. Owen demands a minimum of £80, I thought that was ridiculous, the show was for charity, for handicapped individuals, and we were amateur boxers. Hamish hatched a plan, he offered Owen a wager, he put down £80 and asked Owen to cover it as a bet if he was that confident, that way he would get paid. Owen point-blank refused to take the bet.

The fight was on, the fight was off, I just lay there staring at a love heart on a charm bracelet that had a picture of Maria and my dad inside each half. I was totally oblivious as to what was going on, I just left them to sort things out, head on a rolled-up towel, my feet raised on a small chair, quite content. Eventually, Owen appeared, he told me he couldn't fight me, he was so close to my dad as a kid, my dad took him to places like Glasgow and London, and that it should have been me. He told me he'd had over 100 fights since he was eight years old. He kept repeating the words, "I can't fight you, I can't fight you."

Owen suggested we treat the fight as an exhibition, just go through the motions without actually really hitting each other, purely a masquerade. I thought hard about it, I took on board Owen's feelings towards my dad for teaching him how to box, I agreed to go along with his plan, I was a bit gutted, but agreed not to hit him. The fallacy that played out in the boxing ring fooled everyone, I never told Hamish, I never told anyone.

The next day, police officers came to my door, they questioned me about the crash at the top of Fishers Road, they knew I'd been there. I always told the truth, so I came clean about the incident that happened after training. Curiously, I asked them how they knew.

"We found your car number plate at the scene, son. We've spoke to the farmer, if you repair the wall, nothing else will happen."

"Yes, I can do that, no problem, thanks!"

I'd got a result, I was happy. I asked Paul McGuire to help, he was a good bricklayer. I mixed the cement, Paul laid the old stones that we retrieved from the field, job done, everyone was happy. It was a relief; I could now concentrate on the Scottish Championships.

My dad went to Liverpool to see his old pal, Gerry Marsden, lead singer of Gerry and the Pacemakers. This was a regular thing; they both liked a catch up and a good drink.

Chapter 34

We had six fighters entered for the Scottish Championships at Coatbridge in North Lanarkshire, through the west of Scotland. I was more than ready, it couldn't come quick enough, I'd been working hard, I'd been sleeping like a baby. A minibus picked us up, we had our own massage therapist that day, he was an older guy with tons of experience, we were all set to go.

On arrival in Coatbridge, I felt really good, ready to do battle. I wasn't going to make the same mistake as the Districts, I was ready for a war. I was intending to leave my heart and soul in the boxing ring no matter how many times I had to fight. All the boxers were gathering around a piece of paper that was stuck to the wall, it was the fight schedule. I didn't care who I was fighting, I felt strong as an ox, sharp as a tack, I'd never been more ready in my life, my confidence was soaring high as an eagle. Hamish told me I'd drawn one of the favorites, his name was Jim Mann, from Aberdeen, he'd been in the British Amateur Boxing Association final, on the telly. I didn't care, it was like water off a duck's back. He was getting it, no disrespect to the guy, I was in the shape of my life, standing five-foot ten-inch tall, I was a natural born welterweight. I'd have to be carried out the ring, that's how I felt, I never wanted anything so much in my life. This was my time to shine, open class, on the biggest stage in Scotland.

We passed some time watching preliminary fights, I noticed Owen Smith had moved up to light middleweight. Was he even a welterweight when he wanted paying to step through the ropes with me, or was he trying to avoid me? I got a rub-down with the massage therapist, then I lay down with my feet raised, I was so relaxed, I almost fell asleep. Hamish suddenly appeared.

"Time to warm up, Raymond."

I stretched my muscles, did skipping and shadow boxing, put on my bandages, more shadow boxing. Hamish slipped the gloves on, we were ready to rock and roll. There were lots of rings in the massive arena, ours was the first one at the bottom of the stairs. Hamish turned towards me. "Up you go, son, it's your turn."

I climbed the steps and bounced about the ring, loosening my arms and legs. The referee beckoned us. "Both boxers come to the center of the ring." Jim was a good bit taller than me; I was quietly confident. The referee sounded off again. "Make it a clean fight, no punches below the belt, protect yourself at all times. Good luck, Jimmy! Good luck, son."

As the bell sounded, I came out of my corner faster than a raging bull. It was a big ring, Jim seemed to paw out a jab, then get on his bike. I tried to cut off the corners I tried to get him to engage in a fight. This was my time, my moment, everything I worked for, it was a farce. Back in the days, you never got penalized for refusing to engage with your opponent, I was scoring shots, I wanted to knock his block off. It was like a scene from a comedy, I went from a canter to chasing him around the ring, there's no way I could get him to trade punches. His jab was like a paint brush. I was angry, Hamish was going mental. The final bell rang, Hamish took my gloves off. "You have to get the decision, Raymond, you were the aggressor, he wouldn't fight you."

I returned to the referee, he took a grip of Jim and I by the wrists. The MC announced the verdict. "Winner by unanimous decision, Jimmy Mann."

Hamish exploded; I'd never seen him like that. He climbed into the boxing ring to give the referee a piece of his mind. He'd gone too far, it was pandemonium, there was a lot of commotion, it toots while to get him out. He got barred as a cornerman for the rest of the day. He had to watch the fights like the rest of us upstairs, through a glass-panelled wall. That was my first experience of the Scottish Championships, I was barely an open class boxer, but I proved I could mingle with the best. I was a promising young boxer, I had serious potential. Hamish felt I'd be more suited to the professional game – there were more rounds and I had tons of stamina.

Chapter 35

I'd been going to watch Heart of Midlothian since I was 10 years old, since I met my dad. That year, on the last day of the Scottish football season, we were top of the league. We had gone on the longest topflight unbeaten run that season, but that run had come to an end. We were starting to falter; our luck was starting to run out. This was a once in a lifetime chance of lifting the Scottish League Cup, no way could we lose to Dundee. Graham Harvey had got George Watters, Robert Knox and I tickets for the enclosure in the main stand. Graham played for Dundee.

Everything was going to plan on the field of play, I even bought myself a mince pie with ten minutes to go. All of a sudden, Albert Kidd scored a late goal for Dundee. Winning the league was still on the cards 'til Kidd popped up in extra time to score another goal. Hearts had to lose by two goals for Celtic to have a chance. Celtic had to score five goals, which they did. I was gutted, standing there with my mouth open, grease from the pie had dripped all over my shoes. We shuffled out the stadium to a sea of maroon and white sprawled over the grass. There were fully grown men sitting crying, everyone looked dismayed, disillusioned and destroyed. The party had ended right there and then.

A week later, we lost in the Scottish Cup final at the national stadium, Hampden Park. These were dark days in the history of Heart of Midlothian football club. No Hearts fan could forgive or forget the name Albert Kidd.

Chapter 36

Maria picked Paula and I up, drove us to Edinburgh Airport. She dropped us off where busses parked at the main entrance. We had to get our cases out sharpish, she was parked on double yellow line so there was not much time to say goodbye. Maria was off like a shot. I'd never checked into an airport by myself, the only time I'd been on a plane was to Benidorm when I was 12 years old. It was a little tricky finding the check-in desk. You were constantly checking your pockets for pesetas, passport and driving license. It was a right carry-on going through customs then finally getting on the plane. Although I was scared of heights, I took the window seat, trying to conquer my fear. What a sensation powering along the runway, the initial lift-off was amazing. The animals in the fields turned into dots as we rose above the clouds, then I fell asleep.

Paula woke me up on the decent. She gave me a sweetie to suck on, she said it would stop my ears from popping. After a bit of turbulence, we were safely on the ground. I couldn't hear a thing. Paula told me to hold my nose, close my mouth and blow. Customs were much different from

Edinburgh, all the guards had guns, and rifles. It made you feel slightly uncomfortable. It felt like our transfer bus had stopped at every hotel on the island, we were the last couple on the bus. After a while of wishing we had been staying at lots of hotels on route we finally arrived at our digs in Porto Colom.

Early in the morning we went for a walk only to discover our hotel was in the middle of nowhere. Feeling slightly aghast, we made our way back to the hotel. Paula was applying oil to her skin on a sun-bed by the pool that was adjacent to our hotel, I was putting on sunblock. I lay next to her for as long as I could but always went for a walk around the hotel gardens. Every day I played a round of minigolf. Paula would ask me to put oil on her back. Her back was so smooth, it felt like my rough builder's hands were scraping her skin.

At night we'd always get a bowl of punch, you couldn't taste any alcohol because there was that much fruit juice infused within. There was a couple dancing across from the bar, they were older than us. The man was strutting his stuff, doing funny moves with a camera strapped to his neck. I couldn't stop laughing, I could never imagine bringing that much attention to myself, I was too shy, and I couldn't dance. Paula and I only had a slow dance at the end of the night. After a couple of nights, we got chatting to them, the guy was a scream. We got friendly with them. They took us to a local authentic Spanish restaurant a short walk away the night before they went home. The taverna was old school, there was an enormous pan of paella simmering outside, it seemed like that was the only thing on the menu. I had never tried it before, it was delicious. We sat there all night, chatting and drinking sangria.

Every day we had been sitting next to this couple from London. The guy wore a knotted handkerchief over his head, he was a right good laugh. I loved all that cockney rhyming slang; you couldn't help laughing no matter what he said. At night I met a guy called Scott and his partner, the couple were from Ballingery in Fife, Scotland. They were quiet, and so were we until Paula told Scott's partner I was a boxer. Scott was right in there, asking if I knew his mate, Andrew Caulfield. I'd heard his name being mentioned, he had fought my clubmate Ian. This gave us something to talk about for a wee while, sipping away on our respective bowls of punch. Paula and I would always go up for the slow dance at the end of the night. It only meant swaying from side to side, in a normal dance I was like Herman Munster.

I'd got over feeling embarrassed about showing off my psoriasis around the pool area, it was really bad around my shins and elbows. You couldn't see the lumps of multiplying skin that had covered my head since I was 10 years old. I always had an abundance of hair, no matter how much I scraped it out using my fingernails.

Next to our hotel was a motorbike rental place. I saw this Vespa scooter that looked in pristine condition. All I had to do was hand over my driving license. We could now travel to beaches up and down the island. Cala D'or was beautiful – that's where we originally wanted to go but the prices were too high for our budget. The quaint little shops, cafes nestling on every corner. The beach was small but picturesque with rock cliffs either side of the narrow waterfront. All the sunbeds were taken so we had to make do with towels. Paula's tan was coming on nicely, I was slapping on the highest sun cream I could find – factor 30.

It was the year of the World Cup in Mexico. I thought I was Frank McAvennie during trials for the hotel team, banging in loads of goals wearing my Scotland strip. I'd also got asked to pick most of the team to play a local Spanish side. I remember picking this guy from Liverpool who was almost seven-foot tall, and a woman to play goalkeeper because she was almost the size of the goals. The night before the big game, we all got drunk at the bar, prophesying an exuberant win.

Everyone had hangovers the next morning, it did not deter us in any way, we were still determined to win. This team we were playing were wearing the same football strip, obviously their club colors. We were a rag tag outfit in a variety of strips, not one color the same. They all looked fresh as a daisy. We were getting humped, but I still managed to bang in a few goals. They were so quick I had to make rash challenges, and thunderous shoulder charges. They all kept calling me Guerrero. I asked one of the Spanish guys from the hotel what they meant.

"Warrior."

Sweating profusely, I spent the rest of the day poolside with Paula. There were no victory celebrations that night. We just sat in the corner sipping a bowl of punch.

First thing in the morning, we set off on a long journey up the coast to Cala Millor. We had to lay our towels down, any sunbeds that could be seen must have been taken up early doors by the looks of things. The golden beach was massive, it stretched as far as the eye could see. I was slapping on factor 30 when this cool dude approached us, handing out flyers for bars and nightclubs. For a moment, my subconscious mind went into overdrive profusely trying to work out a scenario that would allow us to spend the night there and drive back in the pitch black. After spending the day on a splendid beach, we decided to make the journey back to our hotel in daylight.

That night, while we were walking around the hotel gardens, we spotted a crowd of people gathered around a soccer table, just like the one I played on against John when I was a kid. It was only 10 pesetas a game. After I got a warmup game, they decided to hold a competition seeing as it was the World Cup. Scotland got knocked out in the group stages, so this was my chance to redeem my country. There were players from Holland, Germany, England, and I flew the flag for Scotland. This table soccer was getting a bit overheated with football chants, screaming and yelling. I made the final against England. I was more about controlling the ball, the English guy was all about spinning the levers as fast as he could. He got lucky and quickly took the lead, I persevered using the same tactics John showed me many years before. It was first to 10, I'd clawed my way back to 9-9, next goal was the winner. The crowd that gathered around us were going mental. Moving the ball from goalkeeper to defense, midfield, and boom! One of my strikers slotted home. He immediately insisted on a rematch, I beat him again. Then we shook hands like gentlemen.

It was the day of a cowboy-themed evening. We were first on the bus that which travelled a great distance, stopping a multitude of times to pick up couples on route. The sun was bursting in the sky when we left, it was twilight when we got there. The tables were long and narrow, Paula got talking to an older couple sitting directly across from where we were sitting. I kept my elbows hidden under the table. I remember leaning over to answer the guy while dipping my shirt in a hot plate of buffalo wings. I don't remember much about that night apart from being overly conscious of my psoriasis.

It was our last day. Paula suggested we travelled to Callas De Mallorca where she had been the first year I really noticed her at Port Seton Pond. When every man with a pulse was admiring her, including me, but I never knew she was also eying me up. It wasn't as far a journey as Cala Millor. Every road sign was in Spanish, but I'd managed to navigate my way around the island to date. We left in the morning after a continental breakfast. The beach was similar to Cala D'or except it was much bigger.

There were people diving from steep cliffs, I had to give it a go. Once I got up there it looked higher than I thought. I was going to dive then the thought of banging off a rock entered my head. There were a few divers pointing out safe places to aim for, so I took their advice and made my dive. As soon as I hit the water, I was immediately trying to stop myself from going too far under. It was a great adrenaline rush, I just kept doing it while Paula soaked up blinding rays of sunshine on the golden sandy beach.

We went for an afternoon walk around the hotel she had stayed at, the pools looked deserted. After a great day by the sea, Paula took me to this Jewelry shop that her mum and her loved, it was right next to the beach. She spotted a lovely ring, I had brought extra money in case of an emergency, but this ring would leave us with buttons. Paula immediately got my attention.

"We could get engaged."

"Are ye serious?"

"Yes! Will you be my fiancé?"

"Aye, all right!"

I fell in love with Paula the first time I saw her, it was a no-brainer. The shopkeeper fitted the ring to her finger and asked if it was a present. I took the ring and placed it on Paula's marriage finger.

"Naw, pal, we've just got engaged."

The couple who ran the shop were delighted.

"Remember and come back for your wedding ring."

Our heads were in the clouds. The moment Paula got that engagement ring on her finger, she wouldn't take it off. We were so happy, so happy we forgot to put petrol in the scooter and broke down in the middle of nowhere. We had passed a garage a fair bit away up a winding hill, it seemed too far to walk. We just stood there by a dyke next to a field, hoping that a car would pass and save the day. We waited for ages; it was getting dark. Then, all of a sudden, we heard a noise in the distance. It was very faint, but it got louder and louder. This old Spanish guy was chugging towards us on something you'd probably see on a farm, it looked heavy duty and had three wheels. The man couldn't speak a word of English, so I had to improvise using sign language trying to point out we had no petrol. It seemed like he was indicating he'd get us petrol, so I handed him the last of our pesetas in the hope he'd return. Off he went into the distance, all we could do was wait. Paula was almost in tears.

Just when we thought he was never coming back, we heard this noise in the distance evoking our memory to that old Spanish guy. He'd only went and returned with a plastic petrol can. Both of us took turns hugging that old man to death. It was the result we'd hoped for, we were home in no time. That night, I went down to the bar without a bean in my pocket. Seeing as it was our last night, the hotel owner bought us a drink. When we told him, we got engaged he bought us another. We sat next to Scott from Ballingery and his partner. When he found out we had no money left he bought us a bowl of punch. It was a special slow dance that night, two young lovers showing the utmost respect for each other. I didn't want that night to end.

It was a long journey home with only an inflight meal and a small drink. Maria picked us up at the airport, we told her the news, she was elated. Paula got dropped off first, Maurine invited us in for a coffee, but when Paula broke the news, the coffee turned into a strong drink. Maria offered to buy the flowers. Paula reassured her mum, "It's going to be a long engagement, so nobody has to worry about a wedding."

You wouldn't have believed I'd been in a foreign country with sun beating down every day, I was white as a sheet. All that sunblock and factor 30 did the job. Paula came home with a beautiful tan, it looked cracking with her blonde hair. That year we walked into Port Seton Pond joining hands. We sat next to each other, and I got the honor of putting oil on her back.

Chapter 37

Before meeting my dad at Sparta Boxing Club in Edinburgh, I left early to buy new brake pads for my bike at the motorbike shop down Leith Walk. The pads were still working but I was taking no chances, you could see they were wearing down. Taking the coastal route, I got lost somewhere down the back of Leith Walk, I knew my bearings though. The street I was on was called Halmyre Street; it ran parallel with Leith Walk so I could turn off further up. I was doing around 30mph, keeping to the speed limit. The street looked really wide, like it was the main road. BANG!

I'd crashed into a car going along Lorne Street, got thrown off my bike and landed up Dickson Street. Apparently, Lorne Street was the main road, it was like a footpath compared to Halmyre Street. Valentine's Preservation Company was on the corner, all the workers rushed out. Marc Valentine identified me to the paramedics, I was unconscious...

I woke up in hospital, intensive care again. This time I couldn't walk out, my ankle was swollen like a balloon. Same old, same old, every hour asking my name, date of birth and my address.

My helmet had come off once again during the fall, so they were checking for brain damage. I couldn't move my ankle. I'd crushed it against the car before flying over the bonnet. I never saw the 'give way' markings that were faintly painted on to road 'til it was too late. I thought I dead for sure. This was all going through my head as I lay in hospital. I must have told doctors and nurses a hundred times.

Paula came in to visit me, I told her the same story over and over. A few days passed, the doctors were happy that my brain was intact, there was no significant damage. I even managed to get out of bed and take baby steps. My ankle was still in pain, but I wanted to go home. Hospitals weren't keen on keeping people that could possibly recover at home, so they let me leave in a taxi once I was able to walk far enough. I fought through the pain and made the taxi rank. I was home in around half an hour. I felt like I had to keep moving or my ankle would stiffen up.

The swelling was going down, so my next objective was getting back to work. It was reassuring I had a bit of money in the bank to tide me by. I was back working within a week, had a limp, but that would go away in time. I couldn't train, though; it was getting increasingly hard to keep my weight down. I'd been in two near fatal accidents within two years. There was definitely someone up there looking out for me.

Once I went self-employed, I could take Paula to fancy restaurants in Edinburgh, like The Witchery and Gordon's Trattoria in the Royal Mile.

Suddenly, one day, I started coughing. The coughing got worse each day that passed, it was starting to get really annoying. I'd cough at work, I'd cough in the house, I'd cough all night. It got to the stage I had to go to the doctors. I was diagnosed with chronic bronchitis and prescribed a course of antibiotics.

Since I couldn't go to work or training, I took the opportunity to drive down to Leeds. I'd never drove that far before, carefully following instructions that were written on a piece of paper on the dashboard of the car. Maria lived ten miles outside Leeds in a small village where they had bought a bit of land and built their own house. With that kind of money, she was still complaining about having to buy a lamppost to help light up the street. After following the instructions religiously, I drove into the cul-de-sac where she lived.

I could tell by now why Rose referred to her house as the one from the telly show, *Dallas*. Her house was magnificent, sandstone bricks, two garages, five bedrooms upstairs, one had an en suite, there was also a huge bathroom with a jacuzzi bath. Downstairs there was a huge kitchen with a dining area, laundry room, dining room, another toilet, two living rooms and an extension that was made into a conservatory. Wow! There were also two cars in the drive and the Mini she promised to give me was in one of the garages – it still only had 8000 miles on the clock. I had conveniently parked my banger across the other side of the road. How in the name of the wee man could she not afford to buy her mum and dad a walk-in shower seeing as they were too old to step into an old, chipped cast iron bath. Greed was the first thing that came to mind.

Tom always sat alone in the posh living room, Alan and Linda had big tellys in their room but would often sit with me in the normal living room, it had a video recorder, the lot. They were still at school. Linda was talking in a broad English accent; Alan was getting there. In the mornings, I'd sit in the big conservatory with Maria having a cup of tea, she enjoyed having someone to talk to through the day while the kids were at school. Tom was always a loner in the posh living room when he got home.

I almost ran out of antibiotics, Maria had private healthcare, so she managed to get another course for me. My cough was not infectious, it was still driving me mad, though. Maria smoked like a chimney, but the rooms were big, and the ceilings were high. She told me she enjoyed my company, and it was great seeing my brother and sister again. I made the long journey home relishing the sign that said WELCOME TO SCOTLAND.

Chronic bronchitis stopped me training for so long I was starting to pile on the weight. The doctor offered to give me an asthma pump but Rose told me if I started using it, I would rely on it for the rest of my life, so I went back and declined the doctor's offer.

My dad and Paula were now pleading with me to give up boxing. My dad was always coming out with quotes like, "You've done enough, son. You've got nothing to prove to anyone, you have great potential. You've proved yourself to me, son."

The doctor told me I couldn't do boxing training for months, so I was in a predicament. Paula never really wanted me to fight, she just wanted someone normal. I was always far from normal. She always had my best interests at heart but this was something I wanted to do, something I was good at, something that kept me on the straight and narrow, in a way I felt alive. She wanted me to keep my looks, I never thought I was anything special. I was a boxer when I met her, where did she get this sudden change of heart come from? She always told me she didn't want kids 'til she was at least 30 years old, she wanted to live her life first. I didn't see how being an amateur boxer could affect her plans in the grand scheme of things.

We had my 21st birthday celebrations booked for the Sweethope hotel and restaurant, which was situated between Musselburgh and Whitecraig in East Lothian. My dad made a big deal of it and had meticulously planned it all.

On the day, he arrived at my door in a brown Audi car with his fiancée, Margaret. My 21st wasn't such a massive deal to me as I was working as a self-employed joiner and had matured way beyond my years. I would go to Margaret's every Sunday to have dinner with my dad and her kids, Kevin and Maxi. A low-key affair including a Chinese takeaway and a good video would have sufficed.

The Sweethope was the in place to go for something to eat at that time. Everyone was talking about how good the food was. The restaurant was lovely. It had a calming, relaxed feel about it. I got garlic mushrooms for my starter, and sirloin steak for my main dish. I never liked puddings, but they were all urging me to have one. I was trying to watch my weight at the time, but what harm could a pudding do on my 21st birthday? We almost had the place to ourselves by the time the dessert came. The lights went dim, they all started singing, "Happy birthday to you!"

The waiter wheeled the desert tray in. I wasn't really paying attention too much until he arrived at the table. My dad's Lord Lonsdale Belt he won after fighting Jim Watt in Glasgow was carefully placed around the cake.

"Why have you got your belt there, Dad?"

"I'm giving it to you, son."

"But you won it."

"I'm giving it to you, so you never have to win one in the ring, son."

"Are you sure, Dad? It a big thing to me and means a lot."

"It's yours forever, son. Now you never have to win one. You can always say that you have a Lord Lonsdale Belt."

"Thanks, Dad! That's the best present I've ever had."

I could hardly contain myself. I was now the proud owner of my dad's Lonsdale Belt. It was an emotional time. I would cherish that belt for the rest of my life. I slept with that belt every night for months. I loved that belt; it was my pride and joy. I literally quit boxing there and then. After chronic bronchitis and near fatal motorbike accidents, there was no way back. That belt meant the world to me, the **_Lord Lonsdale Belt_**. I never let it out my sight, apart from when I was working. It's something I wanted since I was a kid, there was no way I was letting go. It was my guardian angel on each and every **Boxing Day**.

CPSIA information can be obtained
at www.ICGtesting.com
Printed in the USA
LVHW051154270922
729327LV00001B/2